William Henry Goodyear

Renaissance and modern Art

William Henry Goodyear

Renaissance and modern Art

ISBN/EAN: 9783743332386

Manufactured in Europe, USA, Canada, Australia, Japa

Cover: Foto ©Thomas Meinert / pixelio.de

Manufactured and distributed by brebook publishing software
(www.brebook.com)

William Henry Goodyear

Renaissance and modern Art

Chautauqua Reading Circle Literature

RENAISSANCE

AND

MODERN ART

BY

WM. H. GOODYEAR, M.A.

Lecturer on the History of Art in the Cooper Institute, Brooklyn Institute, and
Teachers' College. Author of "Ancient and Modern History," "A
History of Art," "The Grammar of the Lotus," "Ro-
man and Medieval Art," etc., etc.

FLOOD AND VINCENT
The Chautauqua-Century Press
MEADVILLE PENNA
150 FIFTH AVE., NEW YORK
1894

The required books of the C. L. S. C. are recommended by a Council of six. It must, however, be understood that recommendation does not involve an approval by the Council, or by any member of it, of every principle or doctrine contained in the book recommended.

The Chautauqua-Century Press, **Meadville**, Pa., U. S. A.
Electrotyped, Printed, and Bound by **Flood** & Vincent.

PREFACE.

THE first wish of the student, who has been introduced to a new and important field of study by means of a summary and closely condensed compendium, is to know of the books which may supplement and enlarge his field of view, which may supply him with a larger number of facts about it, and bring him nearer to the individual lives and historic details which the space available for a summary compendium is insufficient to include. Not the least important matter of this work will, therefore, be the hints here and there scattered through it as to such further source of information. The "Suggestions in Aid of Reading," which I have compiled for the special course in Art History of the Chautauqua Literary and Scientific Circle, would furnish a number of additional references, among which historical works, as distinct from those specially devoted to art, have received considerable attention. The English author who has made a specialty of the historic Renaissance is Symonds. Jacob Burckhardt's "Civilization of the Renaissance," translated from the German by Middlemore, is a pithier, more philosophical, and much shorter work. I should not wish to urge its use to the exclusion of Symonds, but no serious student can afford to forego the knowledge of it. It may be said in general that the wider one's knowledge of history and literature, the more interesting does the art of the Renaissance become; and, conversely, that there is no better introduction to the study of modern history and modern literature at large than the study of this art. Of all histories of English Literature, Taine's is the one

which keeps closest in touch with the point of view which
recognizes Renaissance Italy as the main source of modern
culture, while Ranke's histories, especially his " History of
the Popes " and his " History of England," are the best
general reference for the sixteenth and seventeenth centuries at large. Fiske's " Discovery of America," and
Campbell's " Puritan in Holland, England, and America,"
are the books best calculated to bring our own American
history into line with that of continental Europe. I have
mentioned these various books from the conviction that the
only true philosophy of modern history is that which moves
from the Renaissance as its elementary basis, that the study
of Renaissance art is the best approach to Renaissance
history, and that the best supplementary reading is that of
the historians whose point of view is the largest and most
comprehensive.

I have to make acknowledgment in this preface to the
persons whose kindness has enabled me to illustrate the
works of recent American and recent foreign artists.
Among these I must specialize, first, the American painters
and sculptors who have allowed me to publish their works,
and the various owners of the same. Mr. Henry T. Chapman, Jr., of Brooklyn, has allowed me to publish several
of his precious possessions. Prof. Halsey C. Ives, chief of
the Art Palace at the Columbian Exposition, was good
enough to give me *carte blanche* in his department, subject
to the permission of the artists and owners concerned.
Finally, I have to thank Mrs. Mabel Rolfe, of Cambridge,
Mass., for her goodness and cleverness in the matter of the
photographs taken at Chicago. The pictures for my frontis-
piece and for all American paintings published were taken
by her, as well as the pictures of Thornycroft's Teucer and
Rodin's Andromeda.

CONTENTS.

v

LIST OF ILLUSTRATIONS.

RENAISSANCE AND MODERN ART.

CHAPTER I.

THE RENAISSANCE PERIOD.

Limits of the Renaissance Period.

THE period covered by the title of my book has had a duration of about five hundred years. The Renaissance had fairly begun in the early part of the fifteenth century, and from the standpoint of general history the beginning of the Renaissance was the beginning of modern times. In a broad and general sense this period cannot be considered to have ended yet. Modern civilization dates from the Renaissance and was created by it.

This broadest and largest fact about the Renaissance is best explained, proven, and illustrated through the history of art.

It therefore holds, in a large sense, that Renaissance art must also be conceived as still continuing. It is especially, however, in architecture and in ornament that the proof and illustration of this fact can be most definitely given. In sculpture and in painting, although the relations and connections of modern art with its Renaissance origins are perfectly definite and perfectly continuous, they are not so immediately obvious without research.

On the other hand there are uses of the term Renaissance

in which, both for history in a general sense and for the history of art in a special sense, it must be considered as having long since ended. It seems then proper at the outset of this little book, to indicate the various senses in which this word may be legitimately used as regards limits of time and period ; observing, at the same time, that whenever we feel disposed to restrict the sense of the term, we have still chosen a title for our book which is perfectly explicit. The period to be covered began about 1400 A. D. and has not ended. No one can deny that modern art and history began about this time. Whenever the Renaissance may have ended, there is no doubt as to when it began. Our title, therefore, covers the ground in any case.

A discussion about words is never useless when it tends to bring out facts. The fact to be indicated then is this: that in some senses the term "Renaissance," either in art or history, specially applies to Italy in the fifteenth and sixteenth centuries, and to the obvious and palpable influence of Italy on foreign countries at

FIG. 1.—Late French Renaissance Carved and Gilded Wooden Chest and Table. At Moyenmoutier.

this time. This is the special and generally recognized use

of the term. Although no one can deny that the seventeenth century continued to exhibit and spread this influence, the term is not so generally understood as applying to a period of history when the seventeenth century is in question. Still less would the eighteenth century be considered to come within the limits of the period, according to the usual acceptance of historic divisions. On the other hand the history of art during the seventeenth and eighteenth centuries enables us to prove without the least difficulty that the same historic influences are really always in question.

As a matter of fact the first distinct break with these Italian traditions in taste, literature, and art, occurred in the latter half of the eighteenth century, and even then it is only in a narrow and limited sense that they can be said to have ended.

The Term Defined.

What was the Renaissance? According to a literal rendering of the word, which is French for "rebirth," it was a rebirth of civilization, of literature, and of art, and according to universal acceptance the word relates to Italy; for we never speak of the English, French, German, or Spanish Renaissance, without the implication that Italy was the original home, center, and inspiration of the movement.

But "rebirth" implies that something had ceased to exist which once existed. The word therefore implies *two* preceding periods as well as its own. It implies a preceding period which was reborn, and it implies an intervening period of cessation, a gap or chasm between that period and itself. The word Renaissance therefore carries with itself a conception of the Middle Age as this intervening period, and a conception of itself as a rebirth of the civili-

zation of the Roman Empire.   These were the conceptions
of the Italians of the Renaissance.

- Now, as a matter of fact, civilization is never reborn; it
continues—with changes.   Nothing could be more different, as a matter of fact, than was the civilization of Italy in
the fifteenth and sixteenth centuries from the civilization of
ancient Rome.   But this matter-of-fact distinction escaped
the perception of the Italians themselves.   They believed
themselves to be reviving the civilization of the past, when
they were in reality only learning from it.   This belief
colored their language, their literature, their daily life, and,
therefore, their art.

In the character of the period we shall therefore gradually learn to separate two things: on the one hand, the
estimate which the time made of itself, its enthusiasms,
sentiment, patriotism, coloring—in brief, the dream of the
Roman Empire; on the other hand, the actual conditions
and facts of early modern civilization.

·The first aspect of the Renaissance was mainly confined
to Italy of the fifteenth and sixteenth centuries and its
obvious reaction on other European countries. But the
actual facts and conditions of early modern civilization
were necessarily controlling facts and conditions for all later
modern civilization.   It is in these two senses that our
conceptions of the Renaissance as a special period, and of
modern history as a whole, either fall apart or hold together.

CHAPTER II.

For a perfectly practical and common-sense knowledge of facts (as distinct from theories about terms, which can only carry real meaning in so far as we know these facts) let us remember what we can of the contemporary history of Europe in the fifteenth and sixteenth centuries, when the Renaissance began and most beneficently flourished.

In England the Wars of the Roses had ended in the exhaustion of the feudal aristocracy and the rise to power of a despotic Tudor dynasty (Henry VII., Henry VIII., Edward VI., Mary, Elizabeth) whose despotic power was mainly used to antagonize the feudal nobles and to exalt the importance of the cities and of the commercial classes. The great personal popularity of Queen Elizabeth, in spite of her arbitrary acts and despotic rule, is the best reminder of this significance of her dynasty.

In France the same alliance of royal despotism and commerce against feudalism was still more apparent during the reigns of Louis XI., Charles VIII., Louis XII., Francis I., and their successors. During these two centuries England, France, and Spain all illustrate the tendency to national consolidation and concentration, as opposed to the earlier dismemberment of these countries in local feudal principalities.

As regards the existence of modern monarchies and modern states, the history of modern Europe at this time, therefore, clearly begins to show its character. In Ger-

many we find at this time the memorable events of the
Reformation.   Otherwise, the great maritime discoveries
made first by Portugal and Spain, the invention and spread

FIG. 2.—Armor of Christian II. of Denmark.   Italian Renaissance
Ornamentation.   First half of Sixteenth Century.

of the art of printing, the use of gunpowder, and of standing armies of artillery and infantry, and the astronomical
announcements of Copernicus regarding the true nature
of the planetary system are to be mentioned as leading
facts of general history.   Where then, the student may
ask, does the Renaissance appear to be a controlling fact
of history?

   To this we might answer: first, that in so far as the
organization of a modern state is concerned, its necessary

basis is admitted to be a uniform system of taxation; and this again presupposes a census, an administrative system, and settled and prosperous industries. Now in all these things it is known that Italy was the teacher of Europe. As opposed to the arbitrary, oppressive, spasmodic, and ill-adjusted levies of money made by the sovereigns of northern Europe down to the close of the Middle Ages, Italy was the country where a census and uniform taxation were first generally in use, and they spread from this

FIG. 3.—Tomb of the Children of Charles VIII. Tours. Renaissance style.

country to the North. The state of Ferrara has been much quoted for its especially fine administrative system. Florence and Venice were also among the foremost in matters of the census and of regular taxation. The diplo-

matic system of Venice was so highly developed that the
reports of her ambassadors to the various states of Europe
are at present our best authority for the history of the sixteenth and seventeenth centuries. The histories of the
German historian Ranke, which are the best authority for
all countries of Europe during the sixteenth and seventeenth
centuries, are largely founded on these reports. What
the Rothschilds are to the countries of modern Europe,
the bankers of Florence were to the sovereigns of the
North during the fifteenth century.* Most of the industries
of modern civilization can either be traced to the North
from Italian sources or were found in Italy in highest perfection. The manufactures of silks, velvets, and laces may
be mentioned as cases in point.

It would appear then for the fifteenth and sixteenth centuries, that while the size and power of the modern monarchies in England, France, and Spain may first attract
attention, their very existence in the matter of administration was due to Italy. It is significant that it was cus-
tomary for the courts of northern Europe during the
sixteenth century to have an Italian diplomatist in their
employ. Such, for instance, was the true position of the
unfortunate Rizzio at the court of Mary Queen of Scots,
although he is generally quoted by English historians as
having been a musician.

In the matter of the maritime discoveries, which are the
most obvious distinction of the fifteenth century, it should
not be forgotten that Columbus was a Genoese, that
the Cabots were Venetians, and that the knowledge of the
earth's rotundity, which was the basis of the search of
Columbus for the eastern shores of Asia, was spread by

---

* For an account of their enormous loans to French sovereigns, see the History
of France by Michelet.

Florentine astronomers and men of learning. As regards the science of modern warfare, we may mention that the first treatise on gunnery was written by the artist Leonardo da Vinci, who was himself a practical artilleryman. Although printing was invented in Germany, it was in Venice that the art found its early highest development. Copernicus was a native of Prussia, but he had studied five years in Rome before reaching his conclusions regarding the planetary system.

It would appear from the above suggestions that even where other countries of Europe seem to have been foremost, an Italian influence may frequently or generally be traced and proven. As regards the general system of modern law we know that the University of Bologna was the great center of legal studies during the centuries which

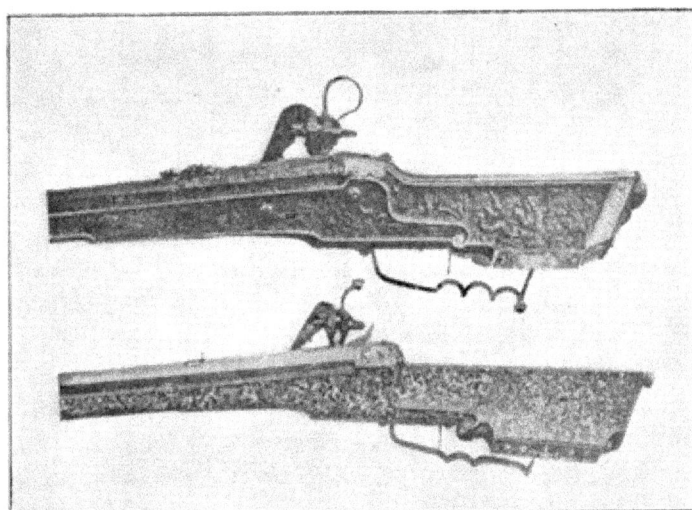

FIG. 4.—German Renaissance Fowling Pieces (about 1600). In Vienna.
Style and designs Italian.

prepared the way for modern times, and that the University of Padua was the famous center of Europe for the study of anatomy and medicine. It is no mere chance which has made the violins of Cremona famous above all others, and that the word "piano" is Italian, or that Lombard Street in London has its name from the Italian bankers who were settled there. It is no mere chance which carries the names of Torricelli and Galileo wherever the study of physics travels, or that the name of Galvani has coined a new English word. It is no mere chance that the finest European palace of the nineteenth century, architecturally speaking, was built for the residence of a Florentine banker of the fifteenth century (the Pitti Palace), or that "Venetian glass" is still a synonym for all that is elegant and graceful in that material. It is no mere chance that the parks of French Versailles or German Schwetzingen and Hesse Cassel were imitations of Italian originals, whose landscape gardening was the inspiration of all modern art in this direction. It is not chance that artificial flowers were known as "Italian flowers" in Germany, or that the lace manufactures of Valenciennes and Alençon were transplanted from the Island of Murano, or that the high ruffs of Queen Elizabeth point to a fashion which came from Italy.

FIG. 5.—French Renaissance Bellows. (Italian style.) Collection of the Louvre, Paris.

For the matter of refinement in behavior, we have the opinion of Dr. Samuel Johnson that the finest work ever written on good breeding was that entitled "The Courtier," which came from the pen of Raphael's friend, the Count Castiglione. For the matter of general education, we have the opinion of Gregorovius, the greatest German authority on the history of medieval Rome, that the Italian ladies of the fifteenth century were the superiors in education of the German ladies of our own day. We know that lady professors were lecturing in the University of Bologna some centuries before the American colleges were hesita-

FIG. 6.—Renaissance Italian silver-gilt Wine Pitcher. Sixteenth Century. School of Benvenuto Cellini. Pitti Palace, Florence.

ting to admit a female student. It is only necessary to glance at the portraits of fifteenth and sixteenth century Italians, which will be found in later pages, to be aware of their intellectual and personal refinement; a refinement which does not equally distinguish, for instance, the German portraits of the same age.

Finally, in the matter of literature let us notice the Italian inspiration of Spenser's "Faerie Queene," and the dramas of Shakespeare which are founded on Italian stories or whose scenes are laid in Italy—then those additional ones (all of the antique subjects) based on the "Lives" of Plutarch, a work which found its way into Shakespeare's

library through a French translation, but which first came
into notice through Italian students.   Or turn to the
"Paradise Lost" of Milton, who had traveled in Italy,
and consider the classical citations and references drawn
from Italian learning.   In the literature of the French, the
comedies of Molière or the tragedies of Corneille and Ra-
cine will offer still more striking illustrations.

It is apparent from these references that the statues of
Michael Angelo, Donatello, and Verocchio, the paintings of
Raphael, Correggio, and Titian, the buildings of Brunellesco, of Bramante and Palladio, are not isolated facts explained by isolated individual genius in the history of art.
They are facts of general history, phases of general civilization, illustrations parallel to those which I have just
advanced in other lines of intellectual activity, of education, culture, and refinement.

CHAPTER III.

IT IS interesting to inquire, for a moment, why the art of the Renaissance has assumed such proportions in the public eye as to dwarf its other claims to glory. Why is it that the influence of Italian studies on Harvey's announcement of the circulation of the blood or the precedence of Italian students in the investigations of political economy is less prominent in the public mind than the frescoes of the Vatican or the tombs of the Medici?

One obvious answer is that modern science and modern civilization at large have far outstripped their first beginnings—so far, that these beginnings are forgotten in the magnitude and wonders of later and recent discoveries; whereas the absolute superiority of Italian art in the early sixteenth century to our own art of the nineteenth century is still uncontested and incontestable. No critic has ever claimed that the art of the nineteenth century rivals the Italian art of the early sixteenth century—that we have produced anything to compare with the color of Venetian paintings, with the figure composition of Raphael, or with the colossal genius which reveals itself in the ceiling decoration of the Sistine Chapel.

In other words, modern civilization has gone forward as a whole, but in its later art it has neither surpassed nor equaled its earliest achievements. The verdict of the modern artist and the modern critic still awards the palm

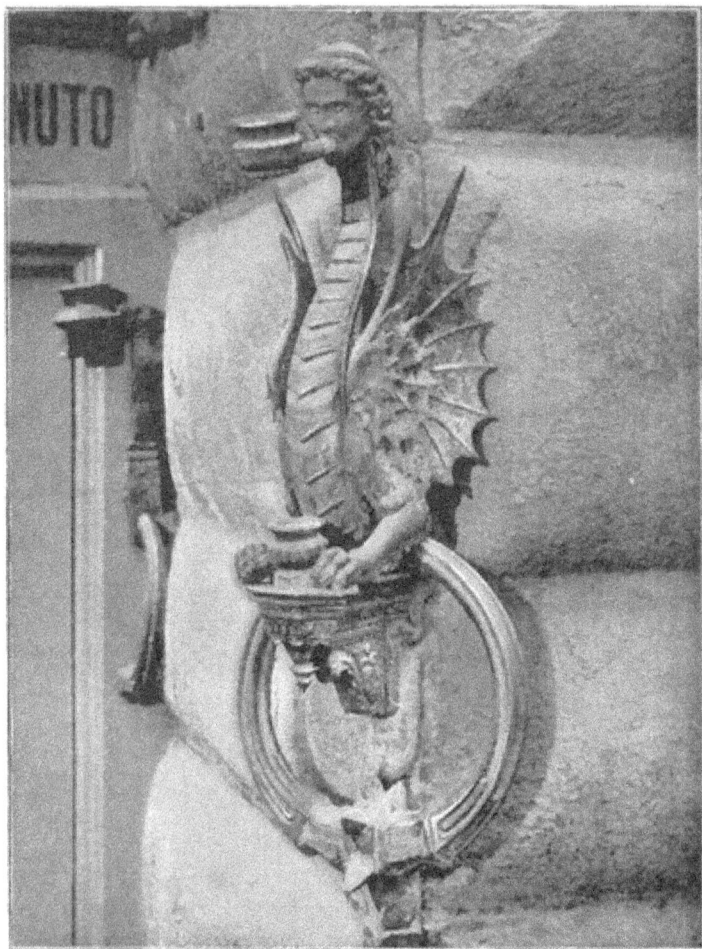

FIG. 7.—Wrought iron Standard-holder on the Strozzi Palace, Florence. By Caprarra. Fifteenth Century Renaissance.

to Ghiberti or to Titian, while the man of science who stands on the shoulders of Galileo possibly forgets him in the marvels of his own discoveries.

One task, therefore, of the art critic and the art historian is to explain the reasons why art and science have so far parted company; to show the peculiar position of art in the Renaissance period, the special causes of its special excellence and the reasons for its later relative decline; but without forgetting to point out that the excellence of Renaissance art was only one phase of a general culture which otherwise has culminated in the triumph of later civilization.

Some further points regarding the relations of art to the public and social life of early Italy have been mentioned in my "Roman and Medieval Art," in matter relating to the Italian

FIG. 8.—Carved wooden Trousseau Chest, supporting the Roman Wolf. Early Italian Renaissance. Siena.

paintings of the fourteenth century, the late Gothic period of Italy.

If we again turn to our question—why is it that the art of the Renaissance has assumed such proportions in the public eye as to dwarf its other claims to glory?—we shall find another obvious answer waiting for us.

The paintings of Raphael and the statues of Michael Angelo can be *seen*. Every traveler in Italy makes acquaintance with them. The beauties of Italian art are

familiar to every picture gallery of Europe. Engravings
and photographs and casts and copies have spread the
knowledge of this art wherever modern civilization has
made its way. It is quite a different matter to laboriously
search for the principles of law, of governmental science, for
the connections of literary influence, to trace out the history
of inventions and industries, to follow the course of social
life, the history of music or of medicine, of diplomacy or
manners. These studies are among the most laborious
known to man. They demand the patience and the talents
of a specialist, either to make them at first hand or to
study them when they have been made. It is partly because buildings, pictures, statues, and decorations last and
are visible to every eye, that Italian art holds a place in the
history of art which only the specialist is able to concede to
Italy in the history of civilization.

But we have still a reason why Renaissance art has been
exalted at the expense of the Renaissance civilization which
produced it. Italy as a country did not long hold the
pre-eminence which belonged to her in the fifteenth and
early sixteenth centuries. Other nations profited by her
advance and took her place. In successive order Spain,
France, England, and Germany have filled the place which
she once took in science, art, and letters. Italian
paintings of the seventeenth century are not superior to
those produced by Spain or Flanders at the same time.
English artists in the eighteenth century and French and
American artists in the nineteenth century have far outstripped the Italians of these same centuries; and what
holds of art holds also of letters and of science when we
compare the place taken among nations by the Italy of
to-day with the place taken among nations by the Italy of
1500. Of all contrasts, that would be most striking, which

should compare the Netherlands of the seventeenth century with the Italy of the same time, as related with a similar comparison for two centuries before.

In other words, special nations have controlled the field

FIG. 9.—Italian Renaissance Bronze Gates in Venice. Sixteenth Century.

of history in intellectual and moral force at certain times. Civilization radiated from the Netherlands in the seventeenth century to England and America* as it radiated from Italy in the fifteenth and sixteenth centuries to the Netherlands, Spain, France, and Germany.

In our estimate of Renaissance civilization we are bound, therefore, to consider the backwardness of other countries at the given time as compared with Italy, but in our ac-

* Douglas Campbell, " The Puritan in Holland, England, and America."—Harper.

count of the reasons why Italian civilization has been
eclipsed by its own triumph over other nations, we are
bound to consider that these other nations have become in
their turn superior.   The payment of a debt of gratitude
to the past is easily overlooked when the wheel of history
has made another turn.

Probably, therefore, there is no matter of more immediate importance to our subject than to understand the causes
which led to the relative decline of Italy after the first
quarter of the sixteenth century, which was the zenith of
the Renaissance.   A natural skepticism of the human mind
often asserts itself above the verdict of the critic.   The
greatness of the "Old Masters" has been often called in
doubt, although never overthrown.   Two things appear
essential to a reasonable philosophy of their greatness, to
show not only what produced it, but to show also why it
did not last.

CHAPTER IV.

IN OUR own time only, has Italy taken a place among European powers as a united national state. Her national existence as a country with one government is as recent as 1871, and even the beginnings of her rise to national unity are as recent as 1859.

It was in this year that the Kingdom of Sardinia, whose main and most important territory was the province of Savoy, began, under Victor Emmanuel, to extend its power over other parts of Italy. In 1859 the territory of Milan was added to this kingdom at the expense of Austria, which then controlled it, by the Peace of Villafranca.

It will assist our conception of the condition of Italy during the period between the early Renaissance and the second half of our own century if we now trace the history of Milan from 1859 back to 1545. Till 1859 Milan had been Austrian territory since the French Revolution. Before the French Revolution it had been Austrian territory since 1713 and the close of the War of the Spanish Succession. Before 1700 Milan had been Spanish territory since 1545.

In 1860, one year after the Kingdom of Sardinia had acquired Milan, General Garibaldi inaugurated a revolution in Sicily which had momentous consequences. The State of Naples, that is all Italy south of the States of the

Church, including Sicily, declared for Italian unity under
Victor Emmanuel; and Tuscany, with several minor Italian
States, followed the same course. This gave Italy her
present national dimensions, less the States of the Church
and the State of Venice.

We will now trace back the histories ot Naples and Tus-
cany to the time of the early Renaissance, as we have
already traced that of Milan. Before 1860 Naples and
Sicily were ruled by a Spanish Bourbon dynasty. Aside
from the time of the French Revolution and of Bonaparte,
Naples and Sicily had been Spanish Bourbon since 1738.
Before 1738 they had been Austrian territory since 1713.
Before 1713 they had been Spanish territory since 1501.

Before 1860 Tuscany was ruled by a branch of the House
of Austria, and had been so ruled, aside from the time of
the French Revolution and of Bonaparte, since 1737. Before 1737 Tuscany had been ruled in the interest of Spain
by a dynasty dating from the year 1530 and the marriage
of a Medici grandee with a daughter of the Hapsburg
Emperor, Charles V.

We will now return to modern Italy after 1860. Her
next step toward consolidation was the incorporation of the
territory of Venice, which fell to Italy as a result of her
participation in the war waged by Prussia against Austria
under the direction of Count Bismarck, in 1866. Venice,
therefore, before 1866, was Austrian territory and had been
so ruled since the Congress of Vienna, in 1815. The loss
of her independence had been then as recent as the campaigns of Bonaparte in Italy.

The final step in the consolidation ot modern Italy was
the acquisition of the States of the Church and the occupa-
tion of Rome as the capital city of the nation. This event
occurred in 1871 as a result of the Franco-Prussian war.

The French troops who had occupied Rome in the interests of the States of the Church were withdrawn for service at home against the Germans, and united Italy thus gained Rome for its capital. The independence of the States of the Church then terminated, dated from the time when the Exarchate of Ravenna was presented to the popes by the father of Charlemagne.*

From this sketch of the recent history of Italy, and from these facts relating to the earlier history of her various territories it results that at the opening of the French Revolution and the close of the last century, her only important independent territories were the States of the Church and the State of Venice, then in a condition of political dotage and decay.

Otherwise, it results from this sketch, that of the three main political divisions of Italy, aside from the two just named, Naples and Sicily were foreign territory as early as 1499; that Tuscany was ruled in foreign interest as early as 1530, and that Milan was Spanish as early as 1545.

In other words, the decline of Italy and of Italian art after the first quarter of the sixteenth century is explained by a loss of political independence, according to dates and conditions thus briefly sketched, and what has been said about the greater Italian States holds, with slight variations of time and detail, for the lesser ones.

In the political downfall of Italy, following the early Renaissance period, we have two turning points of decisive import: the sack of Rome by the army of Charles V. in 1527, the siege of Florence and consequent downfall of Tuscany in 1529 and 1530. All other events are merely matters of detail in comparison with these. In 1527, through the sack of Rome, the popes were obliged to

* " Roman and Medieval Art," p. 116.

abandon the task they had set themselves—of defending
Italy from foreign invasion. In 1530 the establishment of
a Medici despotism over the State of Florence (Tuscany)
sounded the death-knell of the less powerful Italian free-
states and principalities.*

Let us now observe the relation of dates in the history of
Italian art to these events. The last monumental wall-
painting in point of
time, belonging to the
zenith of the Italian
Renaissance, was
Michael Angelo's
"Last Judgment."
This was begun in
1534; the painter, Cor-
reggio, died in the
same year. Raphael
died in 1520 and Le-
onardo da Vinci died
in 1519. We cannot
point to any important
school or artist of the
zenith of the Italian
Renaissance after 1534,
outside of the school
of Venice, whose per-
fection lasted for some
time longer. We also

FIG. 10.—French Renaissance Doorway at
Frejus (Southern France.)

note that Venice was the one important State of Italy which
had preserved its independence after this time. In the
architecture and decoration of Renaissance style, we trace
a rapid contemporaneous decline. In the sculpture of the

* Grimm's " Life of Michael Angelo " offers an excellent account of these events.

Renaissance we follow the same course and tendency.

In the philosophy of our subject, then, we follow the lead of all great writers and critics in connecting the greatest development of Italian art with a period of then unexampled commercial prosperity, which the country enjoyed between 1300 and 1530—and with the existence of a series of small but vigorous and stirring principalities, republics, and free-states, whose small dimensions allowed and favored a wonderful development and assertion of individual character, whose very rivalries and contentions contributed to a production of works of art in which each little state strove to surpass its neighbors.*

In the philosophy of our subject we again agree with greater authorities in connecting the first decline of Italian Renaissance art with the political overthrow of the small Italian principalities and free-states. But this political downfall of the Italian communities has a deeper significance for social history, both in Italy and in northern Europe, than might be imagined. When its obvious causes are sought for they appear to be the weakness of small states divided by jealousies and unable to unite against a foreign foe (France or Spain, as the case might be) of greater military power. Undoubtedly the Italian States were small and divided one against the other. Undoubtedly the Italians had grown effeminate through over-civilization, by contrast with the more brutal soldiery and larger standing armies of the North—but the essential fact remains that Italy became the battle-ground of Europe in the early sixteenth century because her territories were the richest and most highly civilized. The essential fact remains that the entry of northern powers into Italy, implies the necessary spread of

---

* For the relations of the artists to these political conditions, see "Roman and Medieval Art," pp. 216-228.

Italian civilization to the North by virtue of this contact.
The decline of the Italian Renaissance at home is thus
contemporaneous with the spread of the Italian Renaissance
over Europe, and the very downfall of the Italian States
attests the superiority of their material prosperity and of
their civilization as attracting the cupidity of France and
Spain and Germany.

CHAPTER V.

In the periods of Renaissance art we thus distinguish two divisions of especial importance—one between 1400 and 1530, the time of development, of greatest success, of supreme triumph; one after 1530, the time of expansion over Europe and of relative decline at home.

These divisions in the history of art correspond to the general facts respecting civilization at large, which the art accompanies, attests, and reflects.

It is in line with these facts that the general art of North Continental Europe is mainly superior in the seventeenth century to that of Italy, although originally derived from it. This seventeenth century art of North Continental Europe again yields in importance to that of England when the eighteenth century is reached. In the art of painting, at least, the Renaissance drew its last breath on the shores of the New World, with the painters of the American revolutionary time, who in their turn had derived from England the inspiration of Reynolds and of Gainsborough. The art of the Americans, Washington Allston, Copley, Gilbert Stuart, and Rembrandt Peale, is thus an interesting continuation and survival of that of the "Old Masters."

It will now assist our sketch of the early Renaissance (1400-1530) to fix a few synchronisms in mind.

In 1453 the conquest of Constantinople by the Turks ended the history of the Byzantine Empire and of ancient Roman civilization. This event is universally quoted for

its influence on the intellectual activity and the learning of
Italy, as many learned Greeks then settled there, and the
treasures of ancient classic literature were, in consequence,
more actively studied.   In 1452 the second pair of Ghiberti's bronze doors for the Florence Baptistery were finished.   There is, therefore, an exact synchronism between
the revival of classic learning in Italy and the completion of Ghiberti's doors, which are the most remarkable
works of art finished during the earlier Renaissance.

In 1498 Columbus touched the shores of the American
continent.   About the same year Leonardo da Vinci
finished his "Last Supper" at Milan, which is the painting of paintings in the history of art; not because it is necessarily the greatest of all pictures, although this might
easily be claimed for it, but because nothing done before it
remotely approached either its greatness of conception, or
its perfection of execution, and because nothing was done
after it which did not owe a portion of its perfection to
the influence of the great master who achieved it.

In the following year Leonardo's patron, the Duke Lu-
dovico Sforza, fled from Milan, as the French, under Louis
XII., invaded his territory, one step in the series of campaigns which thirty years later terminated in the political
downfall of Italy.   Most of the greatest Italian paintings
belong to the intervening time.   In 1501 Ferdinand the
Catholic, of Spain, conquered the territory of Naples and
Sicily, that is all Italy south of the States of the Church.

In 1509 Henry VIII. of England succeeded his father.
In 1506 Pope Julius II. began the erection of St. Peter's
Church, at Rome, the greatest building of the Renaissance.
In 1508 the ceiling frescoes of the Sistine Chapel were be-
gun by Michael Angelo, and the frescoes of the Vatican
Palace were begun by Raphael.

In 1521 Luther attended the Diet of Worms, and the great wars began in Italy between France and Spain for the leadership of Europe and the mastery of Milan. Raphael died one year, and Da Vinci died two years before these events.

In 1527 and 1530 respectively, occurred the sack of Rome and the capitulation of Florence. None of the greater Italian painters survived these events more than a few years —excepting Michael Angelo and the artists of the Venetian school. In Vasari's " Lives of the Artists," our one great original authority for artists' biographies in Italy, it is of great interest to follow the fortunes and work of the various painters as affected by the sack of Rome, and their consequent dispersion and failing fortunes.

According to foregoing dates the zenith of the Italian Renaissance dates between the completion of the " Last Supper," 1498, and the beginning of the " Last Judgment," 1534.

CHAPTER VI.

THE TRAITS OF RENAISSANCE ARCHITECTURE.

I HAVE endeavored to indicate some various answers to the question, "What was the Renaissance?" but we have not yet penetrated beneath the surface or touched the heart of the matter. In fact, until we take up its art in individual examples, it would be difficult to fix the real character of the time.

So far, in the illustrations scattered throughout preceding pages, my idea has been to show, through forms, ornament, furniture, details of buildings, and the like, the general influence of Italian Renaissance civilization on foreign countries and the rest of Europe, from the point of view that the object which can be seen represents a wider influence in science, manners, laws, and culture.

Comparison with following illustrations from Italy will indicate the relation and dependence of this art, and, therefore, of the attendant civilization, on the Italian.

It often happens that a superficial fact represents and implies an underlying current, a hidden spring of power, a deep-seated motive and cause. Thus it is with the architecture and ornament of this historic period, whose lasting historic influence on every phase of modern life is still attested by the "brownstone fronts" of New York City, by the new Parliament House of Berlin, by the Opera House of Paris, by the City Halls of New York, of Philadelphia and Chicago, by countless public and business

FIG. 11.—Room in the Chateau of Oyron. French Renaissance.

buildings in every city of Europe and America, and by the
terminal ornaments of many bedsteads and bureaus of ordinary fashion down to the year 1870.

I have in my "Roman and Medieval Art" given some
account of the "Italian Gothic" architecture, of its repug-
nance to the usual appearance and natural principles of the
Gothic of northern Europe, of its remarkable versatility of
appearance, combined with constant rejection of what we
know as Gothic character. In this rejection of the Gothic
by the so-called "Italian Gothic," we have a prophecy of
the character of the Renaissance, whose leading feature
was outspoken reaction against the ideals, tastes, and habits
of the Middle Ages.

In northern Europe the overthrow of the Gothic art was
violent, revolutionary, and essentially sudden. It was displaced by the Italian architectural style and art now known
as the Renaissance, and the Gothic rapidly tended to disappear after the opening of the sixteenth century in favor of
this Italian style, and ultimately disappeared entirely.

Some English buildings of the middle seventeenth century are among the latest to show Gothic character, and
England, by virtue of her remote and insular position, was
the last country, aside from Russia, to yield completely to
the Italianizing movement, which naturally reached her
through intermediate countries.

The spread of this Italian style to the north was simply
one result of a diffusion of Italian taste and culture which
carried with itself a particular architectural style. In other
words, the history of Renaissance architecture in northern
Europe is a secondary fact, conveying a much larger fact in
social life and general history—some of whose phases I
have briefly mentioned in preceding pages. But although
the history of architecture belongs to a series of secondary

facts, it is, notwithstanding, a visible and ocular illustration of this larger fact of greater importance: that the ideals, tastes, and habits of medieval Europe were displaced and overthrown by a wave of Italian culture and Italian civilization.

At bottom, it was a question in northern Europe of the comforts and luxuries which were mainly unknown to the Middle Ages—the use of window glass or of carpets, a better table, more garden vegetables, greater refinement of manners, more intellectual activity, less rude hunting and warfare, more music and books, more luxurious furniture, more fashionable clothes, more comfortable houses, and the like. All these various refinements of living spread from Italy and carried with themselves tastes of decoration and architectural style, which also were Italian.

A great assistance to the knowledge of our subject at large is, consequently, some specific information as to the general backwardness of northern Europe, as compared with Italy for the given time. For American and English readers the best work on this subject is Douglas Campbell's "Puritan in Holland, England, and America." When we understand that even an English queen had to send to the Netherlands for a salad; when we can fix the date when starched and properly laundried linen was first procurable in England, and how it came there; or the time when window glass was generally introduced from the Continent— it is much easier to appreciate the gradual flow and gradual introduction into northern Europe of the ordinary refinements and comforts of modern life from Italy. It is true that Campbell's book solely concerns the contrast between England and the Netherlands, but it none the less graphically portrays the condition of England at this time; and what holds at one time, and in some particulars for England as against the Netherlands, holds at slightly earlier dates and in other particulars for northern Europe in general as against Italy.

It is not difficult to understand, therefore, why an Italian architecture should have so completely overrun northern Europe, and why its traditional repetition should have lasted to our own day. It is not quite so immediately obvious why the style whose dominant features are illustrated in these pages should have sprung up in Italy itself.

FIG. 12.—Renaissance Pediment, Entablature, and "Engaged" Columns. Equitable Building, New York.

In so far as we have attempted to describe Italian civilization of the Renaissance, it has been by emphasizing its modern character and by asserting the absence of this modern quality in northern Europe before Italian influence introduced it there. Why, then, should this modern quality have disguised itself in Italy by that imitation of ancient Roman art and architecture which is the one essential feature of the Renaissance style? Before answering this question, let us verify this essential feature in details and by examples (Figs. 12-29, inclusive).

In its developed examples we specify as the most obvious characteristic of the Renaissance style the use of the "Greek Orders," and of the classic columns, capitals, and details as continued by the Roman Empire; the regular or frequent employment of the "engaged" columns and "engaged" entablatures, that is, of the simulated Greek colonnades familiar on Roman ruins; and the gable-shaped or curved pediments, likewise familiar as decorations over niches in Roman art, and originally borrowed from the construction of the front of a Greek temple. (In this derivation we do not include the curved pediment as having been directly borrowed from Greek forms; this is a Roman decorative variant of the gable-shaped pediment.)*

Otherwise we emphasize in Renaissance surface ornament a revival of the scroll ornaments, "honeysuckles," anthemions, lotus trefoils, egg-and-dart mouldings, and "acanthus" ornaments; of the griffins, masks, cupids, and tritons, which were the decorative stock in trade of the later Greeks and their Ro-

FIG. 13.—" Brownstone Front." New York.

man copyists. The "bead mouldings," guilloche, and meander (key pattern or Greek fret), and rosette are also constant or familiar ornaments of the Renaissance copies of the Greco-Roman patterns.†

---

* For the pediment, see " Roman and Medieval Art," Figs. 19 and 21. For illustrations of " engaged " columns and entablatures, see its Figs. 11, 18, 19. For theRoman use of Greek architectural " Orders " and ornamental details, see also the architectural illustrations of Chapter VI., of the same work.

† See illustration p. 51, " Roman and Medieval Art." The most important series of illustrations for these ornamental details will be found in " Greek Architecture and Sculpture," Chautauqua Series, pp. 47-58. All these Greek ornaments were handed down to the Roman architecture and were thence borrowed by the Renaissance. See also Figs. 1, 23, 38, same work, and all its illustrations for the "Orders," capitals, bases, etc.

Let us finally lay especial stress on the revival of the round arch and the entire abandonment of its pointed form. This again was due to the Roman influence.

In the matter of these various details which specify Re-

FIG. 14.—French Renaissance Detail. House of Agnes Sorel, Orleans.

naissance style in architecture, the greatest difficulty of the learner is his great familiarity with their constant repetitions in nineteenth century use. This seems a strange assertion and yet it is strictly true. It is not always easy to understand that with which we are most closely in contact. The constant traditional repetition of Renaissance pediments in furniture, of Renaissance ornamental details in street cars or on silverware, of Renaissaince pediments, "engaged" columns and entablatures to be everywhere seen on public and private buildings, cultivates a presumption that such details are a necessary feature of our surroundings, a matter-of-course appearance. As now used they have generally lost the artistic quality which they once possessed, either of composition or execution or both. To indicate some distinctions between the average Renaissance forms of our own art and the first Italian originals is one important task of my book, and is best apparent from the illustrations themselves. These modern traditional repetitions rarely attract the eye by the beauty of the older originals, and by force of constant repetition they have become common-place—unnoticed because they are too familiar.

We have then, as learners, two distinct points of view and two points *in* view. One is to grasp the great lesson of modern history involved in this constant repetition—the lesson that our civilization still carries with itself this mute witness and evidence of its Italian origin and coloring. On the other hand our effort must be to place ourselves at a point of view where these architectural ornaments and forms would be an absolute novelty, to conceive the time when they were unknown and unfamiliar, and then finally to grasp the causes which led to their re-adoption and exclusive use.

Whatever may be the facts of to-day, the eye of Europe in the Middle Ages was not accustomed to Greco-Roman forms in art. In Spain, France, Germany, or Britain, the Roman ruins were even then so rare, although they have become rarer since, that any knowledge of them, even in an antiquarian sense, was out of question. In Italy Roman ruins were no rarity, and in Rome they were abundant, but the idea of copying their architecture never suggested itself to an Italian of the Middle Age. That antiquarian and historic interest in relics of the past which is so natural to us, is an interest which dates from the Renaissance. To the Middle Age the ruin was a quarry; nothing more. This was its use and interest until the ruin disappeared, and another was sought to be destroyed in its turn.

We have then this problem.   For a thousand years, from
the fifth to the fifteenth century, the Roman ruins of Italy,
and especially of the city of Rome itself, were an even
more familiar feature of the daily surroundings of the
people than they are to-day (for many have been destroyed
since the fifteenth century, and even the use of the Colos-
seum as a quarry was not stopped till the eighteenth century) yet no one had taken an interest in them.   Least of
all had any architect undertaken to transplant their ornaments, and their constructive details, to a modern building.
Then, about the middle of the fifteenth century we find

FIG. 15.—So-called Temple of Saturn, Rome, and Arch of Septimius Severus.
Renaissance Church in the background.

new buildings in which every ornamental detail and many
constructional forms are directly borrowed from the Roman
ruins.   By the beginning of the sixteenth century it is

impossible to point to any Italian building which does not show their influence.   Half a century later and all which make pretensions to architectural effects are borrowers from end to end and from top to bottom of Greco-Roman details.

To comprehend the sweeping character of the revolution in art and history which had thus taken place, we need above all to familiarize the eye with the appearance of the northern medieval or Italian Gothic buildings which preceded.   Our present illustrations are too precious to be allotted to these earlier buildings.   None the less must the reader bear them constantly in mind and make use of all accessible illustration for them.*

Examine the house, the castle, and the church of the Middle Age—first in northern Europe. The house was a plain but picturesque utilitarian structure; often showing its timber framework, which thus became at once a decorative and constructive feature, often with overhanging upper stories—thus economizing ground space,

FIG. 16.—Renaissance Villa near Vicenza by Palladio, with Greco-Roman portico. Sixteenth Century.

enlarging upper rooms, and contributing to picturesque effect.   The castle was a stern and massive pile of masonry. The church was a miracle of stone lace-work, of lofty spires, pointed pinnacles, rising buttresses, grotesque gargoyles,

* " Roman and Medieval Art," type of the house, Fig. 122; type of the castle, Fig. 120.   Compare all its illustrations for Gothic and Italian Gothic churches.

furrowed piers, stained-glass windows, and sculptured door-ways. In the great town halls of Flanders or of northern France we find such details transferred also to the secular public buildings.

Compare the Italian Renaissance buildings. The frowning castle is displaced by a mansion, a country-seat, a villa, a palace, or a university. It is not only in the appearance, but in the uses and purposes of buildings, that we find a change. As regards secular architecture and private architecture, we have an enormous revolution in society thus implied.

Fig. 17.—"Temple of St. Peter," in the Cloister of S. Pietro in Montorio, Rome. (Greco-Roman Colonnade.) By Bramante, 1502.

plied. The decorative exteriors of domestic architecture and private buildings are one sign of that modern life in Italy which was then beginning there.

In the private dwellings of Italy we begin, then, to recognize the modern mansion as distinct from the picturesque but generally unadorned house of the medieval burgher. In churches, the Italian could not abandon the Gothic dizzy interior altitude, the deeply furrowed and clustered pier, or the series of exterior perpendicular buttresses with crowning pinnacles, because in the Italian Gothic he had already rejected them. What he did abandon was the pointed arch, which the Italian Gothic had in common with the North, the exterior panelling in horizontal stripes, or in lozenges, of vari-colored masonry and the beautiful decorative details which he had himself worked over and adopted from the northern Gothic. What he introduced we have already said was the classic "Orders"; columns, entablatures, niche, door, and window pediments, and the whole catalogue of ancient Greco-Roman ornaments.

CHAPTER VII.

WE HAVE pointed out that the change from Gothic to Renaissance style was mainly an abrupt and sudden one in northern Europe, whereas the Italian Gothic had foreshadowed, at least in a negative way, the dislike for medieval art forms which the Renaissance openly proclaimed. It is also understood that the Renaissance style appeared in northern Europe at a relatively later date, and after the fashion was distinctly established in Italy.

As distinct from the more formal and abrupt introduction of this architectural style in the North, the growth of Renaissance style in Italy was gradual and tentative at first, and in the details of carved ornament of the Italian Gothic we can detect many anticipations of the classic influence which ultimately became a constant formula. We will not, however, just yet deal with the actual historic beginnings or tentative features of the early Renaissance. We will rather accept it in ultimate forms and fixed and definite character, in order to meet the question so far unanswered: "What was the cause of its introduction? Why did the first modern nation of Europe turn back to Roman antiquity for its ideas of art in architecture?"

Strangely enough the answer does not begin with architectural history. On the contrary it appeals to the history of literature. And the appeal to literature goes back to the elementary facts regarding the modern features of Renaissance civilization which I have already sketched; but in a somewhat roundabout and novel fashion.

Let us return to our starting point and elementary position that Italy, in the fourteenth and fifteenth centuries, had reached a phenomenal degree of material prosperity, of comfort, of l u x u r y, and of refinement. With this condition the Italian had to contrast; first, the contemporary condition of northern medieval and feudal Europe; second, his own previous medieval condition. Both of these contrasts were to his thinking, to the disadvantage of the Germanic element in medieval history. The empire of Rome in western Europe had been overthrown by invasions of German tribes, and the Italian had since that time

FIG. 18.—Early French Renaissance. (Engaged classic columns.) Chateau d'Usson at Echebrune.

justly conceived of northern Europe as Germanic, or as he termed it, using the name of one German tribe for all—''Gothic.''

In our days the memory that medieval Spain dates from the invasions of Visigothic Germans, that medieval France dates from the invasion of Frankish and Burgundian Germans, is not so distinct, unless it be to the professional historian, as it was to the Italian of the fourteenth and fifteenth centuries. He knew well that the desolation, barbarism, pillage, and downfall that had overwhelmed Roman Europe and his own country in the fifth century after Christ, were the work of the "Goths," as he termed them. Both the West-Goths (Visigoths) and East-Goths (Ostrogoths) had actually pillaged Italy, and although she had suffered more from the barbaric Lombard Germans who subsequently settled there, the word "Goth" kept alive the memory of all these injuries. The very word "Gothic," as still applied to northern architecture, was originally used by the Italians and used by them as a term of reproach and contempt, as we should say "barbarian."*

For Italian conception the Middle Age was "Gothic," that is to say Germanic, in origin and character. When the period of barbarism, or of depressed civilization, in Italy had been lived down; when refinement, culture, and prosperity had returned, two results were natural—a revived interest in that national past, of the time of the Roman Empire, when refinement, culture, and prosperity had also prevailed; and a consciousness of national superiority to the ruder and rougher traits of contemporary northern Europe.

With wealth and leisure came the cultivation of literary tastes and habits; the language of the Italian was itself a modified Latin, and to him the study of the ancient Latin offered no great difficulties. The learning which had so far slumbered in the monasteries or which had been confined to superior prelates of the church, was opened to the laity and the nation at large.

Italian poets and authors like Dante, Petrarch, and Boccaccio, had already in the fourteenth century awakened a taste for reading, but they did not suffice to meet the pop-

* " Roman and Medieval Art," p. 159.

ular demand. The Latin authors were now at hand to
meet it. National patriotism, the revived memory of ancient glories when Rome and Italy had led the world, combined with that appreciation for the refinement, simplicity,
and vigor of the ancient Latin literature which has always
since been felt by the cultivated man of letters and which
the Italian felt most warmly because he felt it first.

It is difficult, when the study of Latin has become the
bugbear of the schoolboy, the ungrateful task of most
college students, and the rapidly abandoned burden of the
college graduate, to realize the enthusiasm of the time
when people studied Latin because they liked it and not
because they were forced to it. Notwithstanding, all our
Latin studies, as pursued in modern colleges, are an inheritance from the Italian Renaissance.

To say that Roman history and literature were studied
critically would be saying too much, but they were studied
enthusiastically, which was something better. More than
this, it must be remembered that the fund of actual science
and actual information was a narrow and limited one in the
fifteenth century as compared with ours. There were not
then a multitude of school geometries borrowed from
Euclid's to take the place of Euclid. The astronomy and
geography which led to the discovery of America were
studied in Ptolemy. Pliny was, in the sixteenth century,
a more important authority in natural history than he
is to-day. As for the history of antiquity, that which we
learn now from a hundred modern authors, was learned
then at first hand from those ancient originals, which the
later modern authors have worked over for our use, and
which we can now more easily afford to ignore.

There were no Gibbons and Mommsens in the fifteenth
century. The ''knowledge of the ancients'' was no empty

phrase to an Italian of that time. Much or most that he knew himself, he was forced to learn from them. The Latin authors, therefore, were not studied then as they are now—as matter of "literature" and simply for literary style and literary training. What they contained was not only worth knowing, but it was more than the time itself otherwise knew.

These enthusiasms of the Renaissance were emphasized, exaggerated, and directed by the influence of the learned Byzantine Greeks, whose influx into Italy we have already mentioned as a consequence of the Turkish conquest of Constantinople and the territories of the Byzantine Empire.

The stamp of the Renaissance was, therefore, a literary "craze," fully justified and explained by the history of the time, but curiously eccentric in many of its outward manifestations. The giving of Latin names to children, the Latinizing of one's own name, were a constant occurrence. We are told by the greatest historian of the Renaissance,* that a pope of the fifteenth century, who was engaged in war with the State of Naples, spared the town of Arpinum from sack because it had been the birthplace of Cicero. Another strange story concerns a conspiracy in Milan, where it appeared on the trial of the conspirators that they had carefully studied the Catiline of Sallust before laying their plans. Burckhardt also mentions the diplomatic controtroversy between the States of Florence and Naples, which was ultimately settled by the transfer from Florence to Naples of the finest copy of Virgil in the possession of the former state. We have also the well-known fact regarding the discovery of the Laocoön group of statuary now in the Vatican, that Pope Julius II. awarded the owner of the ground on which it was found an annuity not only payable

---

* Burckhardt, "Civilization of the Renaissance in Italy" (Macmillan).

for life but hereditary in the family. This extraordinary reward appears to have been mainly due to the fact that the group is mentioned by Pliny as having been considered the finest work of sculpture in ancient Rome.

Nor did this "craze" stop at literature or at eccentricities which have an obvious literary bearing. The re-awakened sense for form and elegance, the dawning distaste for the grotesque but imaginative art of the Middle Ages, did not stop with exalting Virgil at the expense of Chaucer, or with preferring Cicero and Plato to the medieval theologians. It applied its own studies in anatomy and in sculpture to the appreciation of the antique statues, which after 1500 were rapidly brought to light from the piles of rubbish and of ruined buildings which had covered them in Rome. At

FIG. 19.—Renaissance Fifteenth Century Decorative Details, borrowed from Greco-Roman. From a tomb in S. Maria del Popolo, Rome.

a still earlier date the few ancient statues which were known
in Florence and in Padua were highly valued.   Lorenzo
Medici founded in Florence a studio garden for sculptors'
studies and the display of ancient statuary (later part of the
fifteenth century); and the anatomists of the University of
Padua had their due influence on the interest which Mantegna and Squarcione devoted to ancient art.

The influence of the Torso Belvedere of Hercules now
in the Vatican, on the studies of Michael Angelo is well attested.   It is said that in extreme old age, when eyesight
failed him, he still caused himself to be led to this fragment
that he might feel and touch it.   In a similar way the fragments of ancient wall painting in the ruins of the Baths of
Titus furnished the motives and suggestions which Raphael
elaborated in the decoration of the Loggie of the Vatican.

Among all these instances of enthusiasm for the ancients,
it was natural that architecture should have its place and
share.   Hence the architectural style of the Renaissance,
as copy of the constructional forms and ornamental details
of the Roman ruins.

CHAPTER VIII.

RENAISSANCE ARCHITECTURE IN THEORY AND IN PRACTICE.

ACCORDING to the archæologic and critical antiquarian views of our own day, an ancient building can only be said to be copied when it is imitated entire. But this anxious and literal point of view did not worry the architects of the Renaissance.

We have seen that civilization as a whole in Italy could not be, and was not, a revival of the ancient; however much it learned from it and admired it, however much the ideal of an actual revival might have been believed in by its enthusiasts. The actual prosperity, the actual industries, and the actual people were and remained Italian of the fifteenth and sixteenth centuries, not Roman of the first or second century.

In Renaissance architecture we are not dealing in any sense with a revival of Roman architecture. We are only dealing with an imitation of Roman forms applied to modern buildings. This distinction between Renaissance and Roman architecture is one of supreme importance, and for the very reason that Roman borrowed designs and forms were so exclusively used.

Rome had left ruins of temples, amphitheatres, public baths, basilicas, and triumphal arches. The Italians were building churches, villas, palaces, and mansions. The general modern use and modern appearance of these Italian

buildings are perfectly obvious to us.   No one could ever
mistake them for Roman buildings.   This was one of their
merits, but it sometimes leaves a beginner in doubt as to
what makes a building "Renaissance."   The only way out
of this difficulty is a wide familiarity with the details of
classic Roman architecture.   The application of any such
detail to any modern building is "Renaissance"; provided
we are not dealing with the literal and exact imitations of

FIG. 20.—French Renaissance Pediment and Entablature; Roman
Doric (" Tuscan ") details.   Hotel Colbert.   Paris.

the original Greek temples and temple forms which did not
come in vogue until the latter half of the eighteenth century.
Since that time Renaissance traits are often found in buildings which are also under the influence of this Greek revival; to be subsequently considered.

There was the widest variety of appearance and structure
in the buildings of the time; it is only by their details, the
fashion of their ornament, and the method of its application,
that we are able to date and recognize them.   Sometimes
the cornice of the building, the arcades of its interior court,

or the pediment of a door, or a window here and there, are
the only indications. Certainly the only satisfactory study
of the subject is that which makes clear what was done
and what was not done before the Renaissance began. In
other words, the best and only real basis for a knowledge of
this subject is a fair acquaintance with the architecture of
the Middle Ages, and the ability to know things by knowing what they are not.

It may be added, however, unfortunately, that the versatility and variety of early Renaissance buildings have not
been perpetuated by the nineteenth century use *of the same
style*, and the earmarks of the style in these later phases
are tolerably easy to recognize.

FIG. 21—Early French Renaissance. Viviers. "Engaged" Classic Columns.

CHAPTER IX.

CRITICISM OF RENAISSANCE ARCHITECTURE.

THERE was undoubtedly in Italy at the time that this style was introduced, a wide development of villa and palace construction with certain general arrangements peculiar to the country and the time, but these arrangements as regards detail would come within the province of the student of domestic economy or of social life rather than under the notice of the critic of art. Each country of Europe had likewise its own methods of arrangement and construction, and each adopted the one ornamental style from Italy, just as Italy had adopted the one ornamental style from the ruins of Rome. In France, for instance, one dominant type of building was a country seat evolved from the older feudal castle. In Germany, houses which are palpably continuations of the medieval fashions were veneered with Italian ornament.

It follows that when we face the historic monuments we have to deal rather with a period than a "style," at least so far as similarities of construction are concerned.

In order then to specify "Renaissance" traits one needs simply the ability to distinguish the "Orders" of the Greeks as they were used by the Romans ; the Tuscan Doric, the Ionic, and the Corinthian (with its bastard variant, the Composite). One needs to be familiar with the divisions of architrave, and frieze, and cornice, and the peculiar details allotted to each member according to the Doric and

Ionic methods respectively.*   One needs sufficient familiarity with ornamental patterns to know the stamp of a classic design.   Otherwise a knowledge of the Italian Renaissance architecture is a knowledge of special historic buildings, of individual examples; above all a knowledge of the
distinctions between better and worse, early and late, which
are to the student of
history the most inter-
esting reflex of the
general changes in his-
toric life.

There is, however,
one matter of especial
importance to the crit-
icism of Renaissance
art, viz.: a knowledge
of the general attitude
of modern criticism to
the Roman architec-
ture which was copied.

It is a well estab-
lished canon of criti-
cism that the appli-
cation made by the
Romans of Greek ele-
ments of construction

FIG. 22.—Architectural Renaissance Details framing a Madonna Relief by Mino da Fiesole.   At
Fiesole near Florence. Fifteenth Century.

to purposes of ornament without reference to constructive
meaning, was a departure from Greek ideals of art and from
the theoretic ideal of art in general.   According to these
ideals the first mission of form is to express and convey
its use.

A column, therefore, which was devised as a means of

---
* Compare "Greek Architecture and Sculpture," Chautauqua Series.

support, allowing of intervening open spaces, is not a thoroughly appropriate decorative member as applied to a solid wall, where intervening spaces are not desired. The significance of a capital is to emphasize by ornament the point of pressure, of a base, to emphasize by ornament the point of support, of a cornice, to emphasize by ornament the roof line. The significance of a division between "architrave" and "frieze" is the existence of an actual stone lintel supporting another lintel, both destined to support the ceiling of a portico. When these various members are simply imitative carvings on a solid surface to which they bear no relation of ornamental emphasis, they have in so far lost their meaning.

FIG. 23.—Early French Renaissance, "Engaged" Columns and Entablature. Church at Gisors.

For the Romans themselves, who in many other ways lacked the higher refinement of the earlier Greeks, we have a historic point of view which does not demand that they should have been more than they were. Moreover, we know that although they frequently overlooked the theoretic principle in question, they did not do so at the expense of general effects of construction. Their construction was

solid, massive, powerful, and imposing, and their use of
the Greek colonnades in surface ornament was not such as
to impair these effects, and was in its way certainly decorative and picturesque. In other words they essentially,

FIG. 24.—Ancient Roman Ruin. Theatre of Marcellus, showing "Engaged"
Columns and Entablature.

according to their own needs and character, built sensibly
and artistically, without claiming or showing the higher
refinement of the Greeks, whose forms they adopted and
used.*

For the architecture of the early Renaissance we are
again obliged to make the concession due to common sense
and to history, as regards the use of the "engaged" columns and entablatures. As for the Italians themselves, it

* For the critical objections to Roman methods of ornament, see Viollet le Duc's
" Discourses on Architecture," translated by Van Brunt.

must be remembered also that they were unacquainted with
ancient Greek architecture, which first came into notice in
the latter half of the eighteenth century.   (At this late
date men of learning in Rome were planning an explora-
tion of southern Italy to study the Greek ruins *supposed to
be there*, as remains of the old Greek colonies of south
Italy.   As late as the eighteenth century it was not known
that the Greek ruins at Pæstum *were the only ones*, and this
shows how recently they had then attracted attention.)   The
virtues of early Renaissance buildings, like those of the
Romans, are also superior to the theoretic objection to the
"engaged" columns and entablatures based on the original use and meaning of the Greek colonnade.   The delicacy and vigor of their ornament, the large effects of mass
and surface, and the practical adherence to constructive appearance, are worthy of all praise in the early Renaissance.

It is in the decadence of the Renaissance that we find
cause especially to regret the use of the "engaged"
column, simulated entablature and pediment—above all,
when their influence on our own modern standards of taste
is considered.

In this decadence the wall column and associated features
became a mania, a tedious repetition, a mechanical and life-
less formula.   The influence of this decadence is shown
in many of our American Renaissance buildings, which
must be judged and condemned accordingly.

The one objectionable feature of the Renaissance style
was that it tended to divorce the system of ornament from
the system of construction; not only because one was
ancient and the other was modern, but also because the
Romans themselves had admitted the opening wedge in
this direction.   When this divorce had been finally effected
there was no bound to the license of arbitrary forms and

lines. The effect on modern taste of the later Renaissance decadence was to obliterate the perception that a general correspondence between form and use, a correspondence in which ornament is consequently used to emphasize or indicate construction, is the only standard admissible in the strict criticism of buildings, furniture, and utensils.

Generally speaking, the division of dates already fixed by the downfall of the Italian Free-states marks the time when the decadence first began (1530). It showed itself in the later part of the sixteenth century mainly by a colder and more mechanical exe-cution of decorative details, by a more formal and rigid ap-plication of the "Or-ders" to wall surfaces. In the early Renais-sance the ornamental scroll-work is more elastic and spirited, the carving of details is bolder and finer, the relief of the projected columns and entab-latures is lower.

The higher the pro-jection and relief of the "engaged" columns and pediments, the later the date. In late Renaissance the feeling

FIG. 25.—Cathedral of Versailles. Eighteenth Century.

of the architect was more fretful, more anxious for effect, less suggestive of reserve and power. For the higher and more numerous the projections of the ornament, the deeper and more numerous the shadows.· These shadows again, when not determined by construction, detract from the effects of mass and the repose and power of the main lines and surfaces of the building.

In the seventeenth century there was an ever-increasing tendency to multiply the breaks of surface and of outline, often of so bold and so forceful design that it is difficult not to admire, even when we feel disposed to criticise or at least to withhold approval. On the whole, delicacy, refinement, and repose distinguish the early Renaissance (before 1530). On the whole, picturesque license, bold but arbitrary outlines, and cold and mechanical details, distinguish the seventeenth century.

The eighteenth century continued in the same tendencies until the "Greek Revival" at its close reacted against them, and for a time displaced them by a more formal, more "correct," though colder, and perhaps equally mechanical, resurrection of the original Greek forms. The force of the above remarks regarding the relation of style to period will be considerably strengthened if the reader will immediately proceed to compare in bulk the illustrations for Chapter X. (fifteenth century) with those for Chapter XII. (seventeenth century). The illustrations for Chapter XI. (sixteenth century) will relate, as the case may be, and according to comparative dates, either to the fifteenth or seventeenth century as regards tendencies.

In spite of the above distinctions and gradations of Renaissance style, as between the fifteenth and eighteenth centuries inclusive, we are also obliged to admit that as late as the eighteenth century bold and powerful composition was still generally practiced and that our own nineteenth century Renaissance has been, generally speaking, the weakest

FIG. 26.— Palace Poli, and Fountain of Trevi. Rome. Eighteenth Century.

of all, both in composition and detail. The exceptions to this rule are mainly recent, and dating from the revival of architectural taste visible in the later nineteenth century.

The general course of evolution in Italian architecture which we have just sketched corresponds, it should be observed, to a similar evolution which can be verified for the Gothic, Roman and Greek styles. All began with simplicity, vigor, and power—all tended to become more elaborate, ornamental, and picturesque—all ended in complexity, relative weakness, over-elaboration, and straining for effect.

It should also be observed that the history of Italian painting and Italian sculpture illustrates a parallel and similar development, a parallel and similar decline.

CHAPTER X.

BRUNELLESCO of Florence is universally quoted as the first great architect of the Renaissance (1377–1446).   His greatest achievement was the dome of the Florence Cathedral.*   The building itself was begun a century and a half earlier.   The details specifying the dawning style of the new period are here confined to the lantern, or small crowning member, which he did not live to finish, and this dome is consequently rather significant for his engineering and constructive ability and his general architectural science than for points illustrative of the traits which we have so far discussed.

Let it be remembered now, therefore, that these traits are not in themselves the first claim of the early Renaissance architects to distinction.   It was their talent in construction which made them great.   The ornamental fashion of their time is a matter of interest, and the way in which they used it is a matter of interest, but the whole is greater than its parts, and these must be considered in their relation to the whole.   Where the Renaissance details appear it is still by constructive appearance and by their relation to constructive appearance that the building must be judged.

The dome of the Florence Cathedral is especially memorable as having been the predecessor of St. Peter's

---

* " Roman and Medieval Art," p. 210 and Fig. 125.

dome at Rome, and Michael Angelo himself attributed his ability to plan the construction of the latter to the lesson and methods of the Florentine dome, which was slightly larger than St. Peter's, although not raised so high above the ground. It is significant for the difficulty of Brunel-lesco's task that no architect had been found for a century and a half who was willing to attempt it.

In two churches of Florence, San Lorenzo and San Spirito, we are able more clearly to specify the Renais-sance decorative ele-ment. As far as the illustrations carry us (Figs. 27, 28) this element will simply lie in the "Corinthian" columns and capitals, the sections of classic architrave and frieze

FIG. 27.—Church of San Lorenzo, Florence. By Brunellesco, 1425.

used as an impost above them, in the profiles and orna-mental treatment of the lines of arches, in the wall pilas-ters and Ionic architrave of the aisles of San Lorenzo and in the classic columns, entablatures, and small door pedi-ment seen at the farther end of this church. These are all imitations of Roman classic forms.

It will illustrate the constant departure of the Renais-sance from its supposed models to observe here that such an impost imitating a section of architrave and frieze, as

appears in these churches, is not once found in Roman art;
but that it is here imitated *from* the projecting section of
architrave and frieze visible on Roman triumphal arches,
where it is always attached on the rear side to a wall sur-

FIG. 28.—Church of San Spirito, Florence.   After the design of Brunellesco.

face.*   In the same way it may be noticed that the classic
column always supports a straight lintel; never an arch, as
here.   This use of the column and arch continues that of
the Italian church basilicas which had never been entirely
abandoned.

We may also find in these church interiors, suggestive
contrasts with interiors of the contemporary northern
Gothic or preceding Italian Gothic.

* As, for instance, Fig. 33. " Roman and Medieval Art."

The Italian Gothic had already broken with the lofty naves of the North in favor of what may be called calmer and more rational proportions. This tendency now asserts itself still more distinctly. A church interior of considerably later date (Fig. 29) may be used with these to illustrate some of the correspondences and contrasts of Renaissance churches with earlier ones.* The correspondences lie in general arrangements and general plans; the distinctions lie in proportion and ornamental details.

It appears from these views that the general plan of older churches was retained as regards nave and aisles, clerestory, and choir. They will also show that Renaissance churches frequently, though not constantly, returned to the basilica use of columns as distinct from piers,† and also that they frequently vaulted such churches when using columnar supports, which the medieval church basilicas never did. Flat timber ceilings were also used.

Fig. 29.—Church of the Annunciation. Genoa. Late Sixteenth Century.

This is the case with the naves of the Florentine churches, San Lorenzo, and San Spirito, while the aisles are vaulted.

---

* For these Gothic interiors see "Roman and Medieval Art."

† For this distinction, see "Roman and Medieval Art," p. 145.

An immediate contrast by the reader, of San Lorenzo with St. Peter's interior (Fig. 42) will probably be the best means of understanding how Renaissance style is defined by ornamental details, rather than by similarities of construction. In this latter church, we find a vaulted ceiling and heavy pier supports as distinct from the timber ceiling and the arch and column. But the pilasters and columns, capitals, entablatures, cornices, and ornamental details are classic in both cases, and in these it is that the Renaissance distinctive quality appears.

It is generally admitted that the churches of the early Renaissance are, comparatively speaking, less interesting monuments than its palaces, mansions, and villas. As contrasted with the mysterious, romantic, and picturesque cathedrals of the Middle Age, which were still being built at this time in northern Europe, they cannot claim an equal interest; although their sense of proportion and of system is a most interesting illustration of the modern spirit of fifteenth century Italy. Aside from Florence, the most usually quoted early churches of the period, in the matter of interiors, are some in Venice; while the Certosa of Pavia (church of the Carthusian Monastery) has the most celebrated façade. This dates from 1473.

In the matter of dates we shall do well to notice those of San Lorenzo (1425) and San Spirito (after 1446) as fixing the time of early beginnings of the style in general.

Before speaking of the palaces of this period we will still confine ourselves to the name of Brunellesco, as represented by a door of the cloister of the Church of Santa Croce in Florence (Fig. 30).

In this door we become more definitely aware of the ornamental features of the Renaissance. We have here the entire Renaissance system as far as one view may illus-

trate it—the antique border of scroll work framing the
door, the antique columns and entablature with its divisions
of architrave, frieze, and cornice, the latter decorated with
egg-and-dart mouldings, and the surmounting curvilinear
Roman variant of the gable-shaped pediment.

All of these details were borrowed by Brunellesco from
some ruin of Rome, in
which city he is known
to have zealously
sketched and studied
the ruins.   The relief
of the saint and cher-
ubs, the cupids hold-
ing the crest, and the
medallion portraits be-
side it, are of course
Renaissance additions,
but the entire compo-
sition considered as a
door is also quite un-
familiar to us as a copy
of anything Roman.
No similar Roman
doorway can be quoted.

FIG. 30.—Doorway of the Cloister of Santa
Croce. Florence. By Brunellesco.

Our nearest parallel in
Roman art would be the framing of a niche for a statue,
and it is most likely that the entablature, with the columns
and the arc above them, were borrowed from separate
buildings (neither of them from a door), and recombined
according to a suggestion obtained from a niche.

This case will illustrate the whole system on which the
Renaissance architects worked, and the very freedom and
independence of these adaptations are their greatest charm.

The distinction which I have already emphasized in general between Roman architecture and Renaissance copies, is thus illustrated by a special example. An infinite number of such comparisons might be instituted.

We shall now turn for a moment to a window decoration

FIG. 31.—Window Pediment of the Doge's Palace. Venice. By Pietro Lombardo.

of somewhat later date in Venice, in order to consider its typical relation to the doorway. The same elements of antique detail are in question, although we cannot specify any antique window similarly treated. A niche framing, or even the front of an entire Roman temple, may be considered as the original suggestion. At all events, we have in these two pediment forms (curvilinear and tri-angle) the motives which ultimately became a mania in the later Renaissance, and whose endless repetitions and variations ultimately became so tedious (Figs. 45-53, inclusive).

What I wish to point out now for the earlier Renaissance (at least down to 1520), is its reticence in the use of these pediments. Confined to interiors and courts, they are sparingly used even there. On the façades and exteriors of buildings they are unknown at this time. Their first appearance and widest use at this time are for the framework of decorative tablets, tomb-reliefs, shrines, and the like. For such uses, the curvilinear pediment was the ruling one.

The later introduction of these pediments into exterior architecture was gradual and tentative. The same point, though in a less emphatic degree, holds of the "engaged" columns and entablatures, which appear in exteriors at an earlier date. It is, however, in tombs, tablets, shrines,

and the like, that they are most constantly and universally found for the fifteenth century.

My best illustration (because clearest and largest) for the later decorative system of the Renaissance in exteriors of buildings is at this time the detail from the framing of a bas-relief by Mino da Fiesole in the Cathedral of Fiesole, near Florence (Fig. 22). The reader would do well to carefully note the correspondences

Fig. 32.—Early Renaissance Capital. From a church in Venice.

and distinctions here, in comparison with types just quoted —the same classic cornice, frieze, architrave, capital, and column. The decorative details as here enlarged should also be carefully studied—the egg-and-dart moulding, bead moulding, leaf-and-dart moulding, and anthemions.* On the other hand, the original and beautiful design of the capital would find no exact counterpart in ancient art, nor should we be able to point to any ancient anthemions of exactly similar design. A similar remark applies to our beautiful detail of a capital from Venice herewith (Fig. 32).

FIG. 33.—Ornament from the Tomb of Gaston de Foix. Milan. 1512.

It is in these capitals, decorative friezes and relief ornaments of early Renaissance art that we find the most original and most beautiful examples of antique influence.

None of these decorative motives are slavish or mechanical copies, as our own nineteenth century designs are apt to be; yet they have all the virtues of the best antique designs; the same elastic and vital feeling, the same sense of balance and proportion. The more our modern ornament is studied, the more its dependence on these early Renaissance decorations, and also its general inferiority to them, is apparent. I have in the illustrations from armor, fowling-pieces, furniture, tombs, house interiors, metal work, etc. (Figs. 1–11, inclusive), given some indications of the all-powerful influence of this ornament on later history.

As an indication of the early date at which these motives began to make their way to the North, and as another

* Compare " Greek Architecture and Sculpture," Chautauqua Series.

illustration of their beauty, we call attention here to the tomb of the children of the French king, Charles VIII., at Tours. This king was one of those whose campaigns in Italy have been mentioned as an instance of the attractions which Italian civilization was beginning to have for the North (Fig. 3).

The inventive and original qualities of the early Renaissance, as distinct from its dependence on antique originals, are also nowhere so easily illustrated as in its ornament in wood carving, stone carving, terra cotta modelling, metal work, ivory carving, textile fabrics, lace, velvets, etc.

The vigor and variety of these designs exhibit a rapid decline after 1530. After this time they are to be found in superior, or at least equal, excellence (for the given period) in France or Germany, for the remainder of the sixteenth century (Fig. 34).

The detail from the tomb of the French general, Gaston

FIG. 34.—French Renaissance Wood-carving. Chateau of Gaillon.

de Foix, who was killed at the battle of Ravenna in 1512, is illustrated as an easily dated work, typical for hundreds and thousands of distinct yet similar designs (Fig. 33).

We have also other earlier illustrations typical for the best Italian work and influence, although some are taken from the art of other countries (Figs. 10, 14, 19).

Keeping to our point, that tombs, relief panels, decorative details, and interiors offer the first numerous class of distinctly Renaissance designs subsequently typical for exterior architecture, we may turn to the early Renaissance palaces and find our point corroborated here by the fact that the interior court is generally the part of the building where we can distinctly point to the antique influence.

On the whole, the palace of the Dukes of Urbino, the birthplace of Raphael, has the most famous interior court

of the fifteenth century (Fig. 35). The architect was a distinguished, though not largely quoted, man, Luciano da Laurana. The photograph is typical for the general interior arrangement of contemporary Italian mansions and palaces, showing the open arcade of the lower story

FIG. 35.—Court of the Ducal Palace at Urbino. Fifteenth Century.

supported by classic columns. On the second story we distinguish the typical classic Roman wall pilaster, but as yet used in low relief and in modest fashion. No window pediments are seen.

The earliest façade which exhibits the classic wall pilas-

ter is the Florentine Palace Rucellai (1446–1451), a wonderfully simple and imposing composition (Fig. 36). The
architect, Leon Bat-
tista Alberti, was the
most famous of his
time, which was that
of the generation after
Brunellesco. His name
is also a much quoted
one for Italian liter-
ature and for classical
studies, aside from his
architectural capacity.

In this building we
notice, aside from the
harmonious distri-
bution of the pilasters
and entablatures, the
extreme flatness of
their relief, as con-
trasted with later Re-
naissance style, and the

FIG. 36.—Palace Rucellai. Florence. By Leon
Battista Alberti. Fifteenth Century.

absence of window pediments (same contrast), also the
fine effect of the distinction given to each block of stone
by its projected setting.

Others of the most famous fifteenth century Florentine
palaces do not show even the modest amount of exterior
ornament which appears here. The most famous of all,
and of all modern palaces, is the Palace Pitti (Fig. 37)
dating from Brunellesco, though not finished by him. The
massive power and simplicity of this building are beyond
all praise. The method of leaving to the outer face of
each block of stone a part or all of its natural rough-

ness is a means to one of the finest effects in architecture, and was much employed by the greatest of American architects, H. H. Richardson, lately deceased. This method was known to the Italians as *Rustica* or rustic work.

The built-in window pediments of the lower story date from the following century, as does the pilastered decoration of the rear of the building.

In the front of the Pitti Palace we see what effects are ob-

FIG. 37.—Pitti Palace by Brunellesco. Florence. Fifteenth Century.

tainable from simple rough masonry; from its contrast with the plain door and window openings, with the sequence of arched openings and shadows, and from the structural emphasis given by the divisions of the stories as marked by the exterior galleries. To these effects must be added that of the larger wall surfaces and rougher masonry of the lower story. These contribute to an appearance of extra strength in the lower story, befitting its relation of support to the upper ones.

In the celebrated Florentine Strozzi Palace, by Benedetto da Majano, we have the same elements of power, the simply and firmly emphasized lines of the stories and the heavier masonry of the lower story. The massive cornice of the building, by Cronaca, is especially famous, and is the one exterior feature in which an antique model is apparent. The Riccardi Palace of Florence is of similar date and style.

These buildings are more refined developments from the older medieval buildings of Italy.* Since they are somewhat massive for modern taste in their fortress-like strength, it must be remembered that they actually were

FIG. 38.—Strozzi Palace by Benedetto da Majano. Cornice by Cronaca. Fifteenth Century.

fortresses as well as palaces and correspond in appearance to their use and character. It must be added that average modern taste is not sufficiently alive to the element of reserve and power conveyed by large masses of plain masonry. Taste has been corrupted by the overloaded but mechanical ornament of nineteenth century Renaissance.

---

* " Roman and Medieval Art," Figs. 145, 146.

CHAPTER XI.

HISTORIC SKETCH OF SIXTEENTH CENTURY RENAISSANCE ARCHITECTURE.

AT THE opening of the sixteenth century the simplicity and reserve of the early Renaissance were still general but gradually gave way to more pronounced exterior decorations, to a wider use and greater projection of the surface ornament, and a more broken treatment of lines and surfaces. The name of Bramante, the friend and possibly relative of Raphael, is at this time the leading one. We shall do well now to notice once more a Chapel at Rome, illustrated in an earlier chapter, and designed by this famous architect (Fig. 17).

In Bramante's Cancelleria Palace at Rome, a still noted building, we find the same low relief of the classic pilasters as seen on the Palace

FIG. 39.—Arcade and Court of the Palace Massimi. Rome. By Baldassare Peruzzi.

Rucellai, the same constructional emphasis on the lines of the stories illustrated by earlier Florentine palaces, the same artistic use of the blocks of masonry as in themselves noble and beautiful parts of the building (Fig. 40).

In his court of the Church of Santa Maria della Pace at

Fig. 40.—Cancellaria Palace, Rome. By Bramante.
Early Sixteenth Century.

Rome, we see once more the dignified, simple, and noble composition of the best period of the Renaissance (Fig. 41). By contrast with the Palace at Urbino (Fig. 35), where columns are used in construction, we have in the lower arcade the pier and arch construction of the Roman time, faced by flat pilasters. In the second story piers alternate with columns to support the straight lintel, showing another free departure from the Roman system which never used a pier with the lintel.

What the Church of St. Peter (begun 1506) would
have been if Bramante had finished or even partially completed it, we can only imagine.   In its present shape it still
dates from him as the first architect who worked on its
plans, but has nothing either in plan or details to show for
Bramante at present (Figs. 42, 43).

The Renaissance was soon destined to take on colder
and more formal aspects, even in the hands of such great
artists as Raphael and Michael Angelo.   The former became
the architect of St. Peter's after the death of Bramante,

FIG. 41.—Court of the Church of Santa Maria della Pace. Rome.
By Bramante. Early Sixteenth Century.

although nothing of the later building came to completion
in his lifetime, except the piers of the dome.   Raphael also
built several palaces in Rome and Florence.   By the year

1546, when Michael Angelo assumed charge of the construction, the cold and mechanical period of the Renaissance had fairly set in.

To Michael Angelo, as already mentioned, is due the

FIG. 42.—St. Peter's Church. Rome. Sixteenth and Seventeenth Centuries.

construction of the famous dome, which was finished according to his plans after his death. But continued changes in plan, all with the general purpose of increase in size, continued to be made and the most famous building of the

Renaissance dates in its present façade and in the details of interior decoration from the seventeenth century only.

As regards prodigal luxury in details, enormous dimensions of area, and gigantic size of its members, St. Peter's deserves all the fame it has won.　The besetting sin of the period in which this church was finished was over-decora-

FIG. 43.—St. Peter's Church.　Rome.

tion—the idea that expensive materials and lavish display are alone sufficient to satisfy the demands of high art.　In this sense we are obliged to make certain reservations regarding St. Peter's, and all buildings of the time of its completion, without wishing to deny its importance as the largest church of modern history; without wishing to forget the wonderful engineering science displayed in the construction of its dome and its imposing first place among the monumental jewels of Rome.

On the other hand, concession of the merit of St. Peter's is not one to be made merely to bigness of dimensions for its own sake. In exteriors, mere size is certainly the least important of all things, if for no other reason, because we can least control it; but large and ample interior apartments will always claim first place in effect and power—and the Italians of this age were noble designers in this regard. The galleries, corridors, and loggias (arcades) of the Vatican Palace are one instance out of many, and the vestibule of St. Peter's offers a fine illustration in the same direction. Our illustrations for the Sistine Chapel, for the Vatican loggias, and for the Doge's Palace at Venice should be consulted on this head, aside from the interior view of St. Peter's (Figs. 58, 88, 93).

The mention of St. Peter's Church has carried us beyond the period of the early

Fig. 44.—Court of the Palace Massimi. Rome. By Baldassare Peruzzi. Early Sixteenth Century.

sixteenth century, of which I am now generally speaking. Meantime, in the first quarter of the sixteenth century, countless buildings of fine proportions and beautiful detail were in construction all over Italy. Among these I have

selected the Palace Massimi in Rome as a typical building
for the zenith of the Renaissance (Figs. 39, 44).

We have in Fig. 39 an illustration of the Tuscan Doric
Order as revived from the Roman ruins.* It is still in
general modern use as a tradition from this time. The
Ionic is occasionally found on Renaissance buildings (Figs.
23, 46), but is far less frequent than the Corinthian (Figs.
26–32 inclusive, and many others). The Roman preference for this latter Order accented its use by the Italian
Renaissance revival. In our own days the general domi-
nance of the Corinthian Order continues as a result.

FIG. 45.—Palace Bartolini. Florence. 1520.
By Baccio d'Agnolo.

In the Palace Mas-
simi it is still obviously
the construction which
attracts and interests
us. In other build-
ings the preference for
antique forms begins
to develop without
reference to the
effects of the building
itself. The door and
window pediments,
now transferred to the
exterior façades, of-
fered a ready means to
inferior architects to
satisfy the demand for
antique designs with-
out taxing their own
invention. It would
be impossible to deny that there are countless fine and

* "Roman and Medieval Art," Fig. 12.

imposing buildings on which these gables appear; equally impossible to deny that they have found their final grave on the brownstone fronts of New York City (Fig. 13).

The Florentine Palace Bartolini, shown in Fig. 45, long passed as the earliest example of the door and window pediments on an exterior façade, but the Palace Pandolfini in Florence shows Raphael as predecessor (1516) in this

FIG. 46.—Second Story, Court of the Farnese Palace. Building by Antonio di San Gallo and Michael Angelo.

regard, and they also appear in a drawing by Bramante, who died in 1514. The alternation of curvilinear and angular pediments on the Palace Bartolini is again alternated by changed arrangement on various stories.

The year 1520 is dangerously near the first decline of the Renaissance, and we cannot but find the appearance of the exterior pediments at this time significant. The first effect of a door or window is that of its entire shadow as against the adjacent surface. The broken lines and surfaces created by these projecting but still inefficient and useless canopies tend to destroy a finer series of contrasts than they themselves create, and the breaks of wall surface which they involve detract from effects of structural lines.

The sacrifice of the main lines and surfaces to elaboration of details rapidly asserted itself after 1530. We find an instance in the second story of the court of the Farnese Palace, at Rome, where the removal of the pediments would contribute to effects of proportion and contrast (Fig. 46).

In this view we also see the high projection of the "engaged" columns, as contrasted with the flat pilasters of the Rucellai and Cancellaria Palaces (Figs. 36, 40).

In their ultimate use of the classic Roman wall column, the Italians strove to regain what they had sacrificed in the matter of surface effects, and of structural lines in the horizontal, by emphasis on the perpendiculars. This was obtained by applying the simulated columns in the proportion of the entire building (Fig. 26), but at the expense of any treatment emphasizing the stories, or other organic conditions of the building.

This disregard of organism is the almost necessary resort of any modern architect designing in Renaissance style and wishing to give imposing lines to his building. To the classic enthusiasms of the old Renaissance, which forced the use of these columns on every important structure, we can make almost any concessions, but there is no doubt that they have laid a very serious burden on the shoulders of later architects who have less interest in Virgil and Pliny, and the same reverence for Vitruvius.*

---

*Vitruvius is the Roman author on architecture, whose work became the standard of appeal of all Italian architects soon after 1500.

The last great architect of the Renaissance was Palladio, 1518–1580. He was a native of Vicenza, and most of his important work was in north Italy, especially in Vicenza and in Venice. Two interesting views of his designs in and near Vicenza are subjoined; one of these is his most famous villa (Fig. 16).

The great merit of Palladio was his disposition of interior apartments and his arrangements of interior plans. In his use of the "Orders" on exteriors he was distinguished by refinement, moderation, a sense of proportion and regard for organic appearance and effect. In his day the use of these "Orders" in exteriors was

FIG. 47.—Palace Marcantonio Tiene. By Palladio. Vicenza.

a matter-of-course formula for every architect, as a result of that literary enthusiasm for Roman antiquity whose peculiar causes I have endeavored to explain (pp. 54–60).

In these enthusiasms we understand the architects as sharers within the domain of their own peculiar art, so that Palladio, for instance, was a close student of the ancient Roman ruins; but it is important to know that the larger basis and groundwork of the architectural fashion was that general point of view of the entire Italian culture and education, in which the literary sentiment of the men of letters,

the historic interest of the student of history, the debt of
the man of science to ancient learning, and the patriotic interest of the average Italian in the former glories of his
country were the essential explanation.

We must not forget to mention finally the name of Vi-
gnola (1507-1573) whose treatise on the Orders has not even
yet entirely lost its influence on modern architecture. As a
planner and composer of buildings he was not Palladio's
equal, but he long ranked as the leading theorist on the
subject of Roman, *i. e.* Renaissance, details. The Italian
theory that Roman art was an inspired canon for the imitation of all later history reached its climax in his treatise.

CHAPTER XII.

DECADENCE OF RENAISSANCE ARCHITECTURE, SEVEN-TEENTH AND EIGHTEENTH CENTURIES.

IN THE latter part of the sixteenth century Italian archi-tecture turned from the study and copy of the Roman buildings to the study and copy of its own earlier copies.

The period of continu-ation and tradition set in, as against the period of original adaptation or of original creation mistaken for adaptation or disguised as adap-tation.

In this period the method and the form-ula, that is to say the classic detail, became the main thing. The building was forgotten in its ornament. The whole became less im-portant than its parts. The beautiful variety and real inventiveness of the early modern Italian art gradually

FIG. 48.—French Renaissance Doorway. Villeneuve-les-Avignon.

disappeared, while the shell of its exterior and superficial appearance continued to subsist.

In illustrating the later course of this movement we shall
find it interesting to choose a single motive and follow the
course of its evolution. We will select the curvilinear
pediment, which we first noticed at length over the door of
Brunellesco (Fig. 30).

The examples of subsequent evolution are selected from
the French Renaissance but will be typical for Italian counterparts and originals.

In the French doorway (Fig. 48) we notice, as compared
with Brunellesco's
door, the higher pro-
jection and relief (de-
signed to produce
stronger shadows) both
of the main design and
of the ornamental carv-
ings in detail; and the
broken horizontals.
This break in the hori-
zontals is connected
with the assumption of
a double plane for the
ornament, in which the
central portion is
thrown forward from
the sides; the motive
being to increase
variety of surfaces,
outlines, lights, and
shadows.

Fig. 49.—French Renaissance Doorway.
Villeneuve-les-Avignon.

A momentous step farther in the same direction is visible
in our next French doorway (Fig. 49). Not only are the
projections enormously exaggerated, but the entire pedi-

ment is broken into exterior wings with a recessed center.

This broken pediment line, also found in the triangular form of the same period, is to be seen in ruins of the Roman decadence,* but it appears in Italian Renaissance art at a later date than does the unbroken form.

In our next doorway (Fig. 50), the central portion of the arc has disappeared entirely. The form can only be comprehended by reference to the preceding type.

Turn now to an entire cathedral façade of the late Spanish Renaissance and we have a type of the "baroque" Renaissance style as origi-

FIG. 50.—French Doorway. Villeneuve-les-Avignon.

nally native to Italy of the seventeenth century (Fig. 51).

In this illustration the entire central front of the building is a built up travesty of our last motive. What had once been the framing of a door or window, and originally the ornament of a Roman niche for a statue, has become the entire front of a building. Meantime the original forms in their original place can be seen on windows and niches for statuary, of the same building.

The sway of this style in all parts of Europe is shown by

*View from eastern Syria, "Roman and Medieval Art," p. 42.

FIG. 51.—Cathedral of Murcia. Late Spanish Renaissance.

the English example from St. Mary's College at Oxford
(Fig. 52), in which the twisted or spiral column appears, as an additional feature. Such columns must be
understood as having been originally in bronze and made
for the shrine of a church, as in the great shrine of St.
Peter's at Rome. In fact, the whole history of the later
Renaissance may be understood as a transfer of designs for
altars, shrines, and tablets to the exterior details, and,
finally, to the entire
composition of a build-
ing. What was more
endurable in the way
of broken surfaces and
arbitrary lines in
smaller and less pre-
tentious objects, or in
more tractable or duc-
tile materials, like
wood, plaster, or metal,
became less endurable
when transferred to
entire buildings and to
large masonry forms.

FIG. 52.—St. Mary's College. Oxford. Seventeenth Century English Renaissance.

In our critical atti-
tude toward the late
Renaissance our point
of view must be
largely determined by the dimension and use of the given
form, and by its relation to the entire building. Although
a doorway like that of St. Mary's College at Oxford
must be admitted to be a corrupt and extravagant design,
we cannot deny its picturesque quality and picturesque
relation to the whole building. From the standpoint

of history it even becomes a most interesting evolution.

In face of an entire building like the Spanish Cathedral of Murcia, where a similar design appears in the entire front, which is worried and fretted from top to bottom with meaningless breaks and projections, our attitude of criticism becomes more severe, although the historic interest still preponderates (Fig. 51).

Fig. 53.—St. Étienne du Mont. Paris. Seventeenth Century.

In the French doorways which have been quoted we must concede much picturesque beauty; given an otherwise mainly plain and unpretentious house surface, as would appear from the glimpses of the exteriors obtained in the views. As regards the element of dimension, where the form is the same, it is clear that the façade of St. Étienne du Mont at Paris (Fig. 53) has sacrificed all thoughts of a serious relation between appearance and construction by the size of its pediments. Were the same shapes limited in size to the older use as canopy for door or window, the building would be the gainer.

It would be erroneous to suppose that the later Renaissance was entirely given over to perversions and over-elaborations of its earlier designs. Much was done that was at least imposing and monumental, and much that was comparatively simple, although in all these cases the mechanical quality of the detail carvings in capitals and surface ornaments is to be observed. In other cases a somewhat cold and bare appearance, owing to the absence of ornament in detail, is often apparent.

St. Paul's Cathedral in London (Sir Christopher Wren)

FIG. 54.—St. Paul's Cathedral. London. Seventeenth Century.

may be instanced as a case fairly described by the general hints of the above paragraph. An instance of this cold but still monumental style may also be found in the Cathedral of Versailles, selected for a view because it offers an available photograph illustrative of this class of later Renaissance art (Fig. 25). The Poli Palace at Rome, with the façade fronting the Fountain of Trevi, is a fine illustra-

tion of the monumental qualities frequently found in late
Renaissance style (Fig. 26).

On the other hand it would be difficult to find in church
interiors any making pretensions to importance which are
not disfigured by the arbitrary and broken lines and details
of the shrines, tombs, and altars.

In its later days the Renaissance was at its best in locali-

Fig. 55.—House in Leyden. Seventeenth
Century Dutch Renaissance.

ties where a simple
taste and simple life
forbade the effort at
extravagant display or
were, by virtue of the
personal dignity and
republican virtues of
the population, su-
perior to it.   Such a
locality was Holland,
and we may find hints
on this point in the
views from Leyden
(Figs. 55, 56).

One of these views
reproduces a seven-
teenth century house
of some fame on ac-
count of its historic
associations with the
life of the Puritan
leader, John Robinson.
This house, built in
1683, stands on the site of the earlier one which he occupied. Its appearance will recall many of the Colonial houses
of our own country and will remind us under what guise

the Italian style of the Renaissance was familiar to our own immediate forefathers.

The Dutch Renaissance exercised decisive influence both on England and on America, and explains the superior simplicity of the so-called style of Queen Anne (English eighteenth century Renaissance) and of our own so-called "Colonial style" (early American Renaissance). The way and manner in which the Netherland influence affected both England and America has been best explained by a book already quoted—Douglas Campbell's "The Puritan in Holland, England, and America."

To return finally for a moment to the sixteenth century period of superior art, let us remember here, also, that at a given date

FIG. 56.—Town Hall of Leyden. Dutch Renaissance. Late Sixteenth Century.

the contemporary building of France or Germany may be superior to a given one in Italy; because as the style moved from south to north and northwest, it largely traveled from point to point by gradual geographical contact as well as by sudden transportation by means of an imported Italian architect, or through a native architect who had studied in Italy.

Hence, as the history of the Renaissance all over Europe

is one of an early period of more spontaneous and vital
energy as succeeded by another of more mechanical and
colder art, and as the movement started from an Italian
center, it follows that the North may reflect at a later time
an earlier stage of the Italian inspiration.   Throw a stone
into the middle of a pool of water, and when the last
ripples are reaching its circumference the center has become
quiescent.   This is an illustration of the course of historic
influence.   It is doubtful if Italy can offer a parallel for the
given time to the sixteenth century castle façades of German
Heidelberg, which it had inspired.   Some of my most significant illustrations, for the vigor and life of early Renaissance Italian art are borrowed from France (Figs. 10, 11,
14, 18, 21, 34).

France and Spain were, by blood and by sympathies of
history and of Roman traditions, most nearly allied to Italy,
and most susceptible of a native and original continuance of
the Italian movement reviving the memory of Rome.   But
of these two countries, France was geographically nearer
to Italy, and alone geographically in contact with it.
Moreover, the French population had a lively, vivacious,
and susceptible taste which most quickly responded to the
Italian influence.   The castles and country-seats of the
French Renaissance are, taken in bulk, beyond any dispute
the most interesting monuments of the style outside of
Italy.

An account of the more recent history of modern architecture is reserved for a later chapter.

CHAPTER XIII.

RELATION OF PAINTING TO OTHER ARTS OF THE RENAISSANCE.

ACCORDING to a philosophic view of our subject, the art of sculpture should for some reasons take precedence either of architecture or of painting. The interest in physical nature and the study of its forms and appearances from the standpoint of nature (as distinct from the use of these forms to teach the lessons of religion and to represent the stories and events of the Bible narrative), were essential features of the Renaissance. A corresponding fact was the interest in the works of ancient sculpture, which also distinguished the period. Sculpture was the earliest art to show that scientific study of design in the cause of nature, which still rules the modern time. The second pair of bronze doors by Ghiberti, of the Baptistery in Florence, begun about 1425, will convey more clearly to the modern eye than any other monument of art the epoch-making and really modern character of the fifteenth century in Italy.

Our reasons for treating first of architecture, are first, that the exterior antique coloring and enthusiasms which have given the whole period its name are most visibly shown in this art; second, that the historic continuity of the movement between the fifteenth and nineteenth centuries is most easily illustrated by this art; third, that the break with the Middle Ages is most abrupt in architecture and most easily illustrated by the overthrow of the Gothic style in favor of Renaissance.

Some reasons may now be offered for giving painting the
second place in our treatment.

Painting in the fifteenth and sixteenth centuries was first
and foremost wall decoration; that is, architectural decoration, in its location, in its character, and in its purpose.
No adequate idea of the architecture of the time can
be formed without considering the adornment given by

FIG. 57.—Ceiling of a Room in the Chateau of Oyron, with Mythologic Paintings.
French Renaissance. Compare Fig. 11.

this sister art, and the magnificence of the interior apartments as thus decorated.

A purely superficial and outside view of Renaissance architecture, both in the literal and figurative sense, is obtained
when we confine ourselves to those traits of the " Orders "
which concern exteriors, or when we confine ourselves to
interior details as distinct from the great surfaces devoted
to the wall-paintings. The most important part of a build-

ing is the interior. The proper treatment of an interior in color offers an even more difficult problem than that of exterior architecture.

As the painting of the Italian Renaissance was dominantly architectural, we shall, therefore, do well to join our account of the subject to that of architecture.

In the matter of the importance and general bearing of our subject, we shall notice next, that the continuity of history, as between the Middle Age and the Renaissance, is best illustrated by painting, whereas the break with the Middle Age is best shown by architecture. However different these periods were, both were Christian. The Italian wall-paintings of the Gothic fourteenth century were the direct predecessors of those of the fifteenth century. The same series of types and subjects was continued.

On the other hand, it is admitted that the Renaissance celebrated its greatest and purest triumph in the art of painting. The perfection of its productions in this art is still

FIG. 58.—Loggie or Corridor of the Vatican. Built by Bramante and decorated by Raphael.

unattacked and unattackable. If in architecture we especially strive to show how the early Renaissance influenced later times—in painting we are able especially

to show how far, in some respects, it surpassed them.

As regards sculpture, we shall concede, however, that the study of solid and concrete form must always logically precede successful representation on a flat surface; we shall concede that these studies in solid form actually did precede in point of time and preliminary importance, and we shall subsequently be able to show that whereas the greatest triumph of the sixteenth century was in painting, the greatest triumph of the fifteenth century was in sculpture.

CHAPTER XIV.

FIFTEENTH CENTURY RENAISSANCE PAINTING.

For a skeleton view of the subject, we shall lay down the following preliminary outlines:

In the eighteenth century great Italian painting is conspicuous by its absence. The names of the Tiepoli (singular, Tiepolo) in Venice, or of Canaletto and of Guardi, famed for their views of Venetian architecture, will hold a very minor place in the perspective which places the sixteenth century in the foreground.

In the seventeenth century the painters of Spain and the Netherlands were at least the equals and often the superiors of their Italian brethren of the same date, a fact which has its analogies in the history of architecture. At this time the Italian painting was still excellent in color, in design, and in science; but it had come to have a more academic and formal, less spirited and less genuine, quality in the treatment and conception of subjects. Its color cannot compare with that of the Venetians of the sixteenth century. Its composition did not rival that of Raphael. Its intellectual quality did not remotely approach the genius of Michael Angelo or Da Vinci. Above all its scale and dimension of productions had fallen. Scarcely any great architectural compositions were produced in the seventeenth century; which was almost entirely confined to panel painting and canvas as distinct from frescoes. The importance of Guido's " Aurora " makes it one of the rare exceptions to this statement.

In turning to the sixteenth century painting we note its most important monumental works as the decoration of the Sistine Chapel of the Vatican, by Michael Angelo; the wall-paintings of the Vatican by Raphael, and the decoration of the Doge's Palace in Venice by a whole series of the great Venetian artists. The forerunner and first great painter of this period was Da Vinci, whose "Last Supper" in Milan was finished about 1498. As leading up to this period we begin with the fifteenth century.

To a comprehension at once of the limitations of this time and of its remarkable advance over that which preceded, we must remember what this preceding time had done and what its characteristics were. In my "Roman and Medieval Art" I have given some illustrations of the art of Giotto, its leading master, and some account of the art revolution accomplished in the fourteenth century and best represented by his work.

This work was the overthrow of that stiff and formal style of design which Byzantine art had practiced for nearly a thousand years preceding;* but Italian painting was still in its infancy during the fourteenth century and was still controlled by the medieval point of view, in which nature for its own sake played no part.

Italian Christian art was still satisfied during the fourteenth century with the most primitive and summary indications of natural surroundings and backgrounds. Portraiture was not attempted, neither was perspective or the realistic rendering of details. Its color scheme was, however, bright and decorative, its conception of the subject matter serious and original.

In contrast with these traits the realistic point of view was the ruling one for the fifteenth century. No figure but

* Compare the Byzantine mosaics—" Roman and Medieval Art."

FIG. 59.—Detail from the Raising of Eutychus. By Masaccio.
Brancacci Chapel, Florence. About 1425.

was drawn and colored from an actual model; no background without a landscape (Fra Angelico is the sole exception and only in some cases); no landscape that did not in effort strive to show the facts of nature; no face that was not a portrait; no expression that did not strive to reveal character.

More than this, the actual Italian life of the time was represented in the disguise of scripture subjects. The drunkenness of Noah takes place in an Italian vineyard (Benozzo Gozzoli in Pisa). The building of the Tower of Babel is done by Italian masons in an Italian landscape (Benozzo Gozzoli in Pisa). The birth of the Savior is a domestic scene in Florence (Ghirlandajo in Santa Maria Novella).

We should hasten to add that the incongruities of these representations soon cease to amuse, or even to draw the attention of, a student as anachronisms. On the contrary, it is the actual life of Italy which he delights to find, as the time itself delighted to represent it.

There is a double point of view from which we learn to understand that neither impiety nor indifference to the attributed subject is in question in these pictures. The literature of the Bible, as illustrated by art, was so far part and parcel of the daily lives of the people that it was most natural for them to see it represented through the medium of their own actual surroundings. The subjects were traditional, and although they had been represented in earlier times with less matter-of-fact detail, they never had been presented so as to represent the life of Palestine.

On the other hand, the literature of the Bible was valued as a species of epitome of life and history at large, in which all periods of civilization and all varieties of costume were equally congenial to the heart and spirit of the matter. The Madonna was not only the Virgin Mary, but a type and ideal of the purity of motherhood. The drunkenness of Noah was the standard temperance sermon. In the domestic life of the Holy Family was found a type and ideal of the domestic life of humanity at large.

What we should then mainly gather from those realistic features of fifteenth century art which strike us as incongruous, is that a dawning, or rather a reawakened, sense of the beauty of actual nature and interest in visible things for their own sake led the artist to create their counterparts and the people to delight in looking at them. The traditional subjects of Christian art were not less interesting, but rather more so on this account.

The first development of fifteenth century art was Florentine, and the artists of Florence became the masters and teachers of all Italy. It is, therefore, by no means especially in Florence that their work is to be studied. On the lower walls of the Sistine Chapel at Rome is a most important series of frescoes by a number of Florentine painters. In the Campo Santo at Pisa* there is another series, the work of the Florentine Benozzo Gozzoli. Besides these we may name as especially important the wall-paintings of Ghirlandajo (Geerlandaio) in the Church of Santa Maria Novella in Florence.

The Florentine Masaccio (Masatcheo) was the first great innovator of his time, and his name stands in fifteenth century painting as does that of Giotto in the fourteenth. Not only was he the first in time, but he was also distinctly the greatest of his entire period, which lasted down to the "Last Supper" of Da Vinci. This position is awarded him not only on grounds of execution and technical improvement of design, but also for the great dignity and power of his thoughtful paintings.

* " Roman and Medieval Art," Fig. 143.

In the Brancacci (Brancatchy) Chapel of the Church of
Santa Carmine (Carminy) at Florence are found the great
wall-paintings of this
master, who died so
young that we other-
wise can quote no really
important picture by
his hand. They were
executed between 1423
and 1428.

From the various
paintings of this chapel
I have selected a detail
from a small portion of
"The Raising of Euty-
chus," in which the
strong realism and dif-
ferentiation of the por-
traits and of their facial
expressions are well il-
lustrated. These may
be compared with the
faces in Giotto's "Dep-
osition," for a contrast
with the style preced-
ing.* Supposed to be
from a design of Ma-
saccio, as executed by
his follower Filippino
Lippi, is the picture of
"St Peter in Prison,
Visited by St. Paul," another of the series in this chapel.

FIG. 60.—St. Paul Visiting St. Peter in Prison.
Design by Masaccio. Execution
by Filippino Lippi.

* Fig. 146, " Roman and Medieval Art."

According to the natural conditions of the large wall spaces to be decorated (see for example the lower side walls of the Sistine Chapel, Fig. 88, or the walls of the Campo Santo at Pisa, Fig. 143, " Roman and Medieval Art "), the most usual shape of the wall-painting was that of a large oblong panel, and this was filled with a multitude of figures of life-size dimensions. The range and choice of subjects covered the whole field of Bible history. There

FIG. 61.—"Christ giving the Keys to Peter." Fresco by Perugino. Sistine Chapel, Rome. (Compare Fig. 87.)

are no similar pictures to be seen outside of Italy, and here they can only be known on the plastered walls of the original buildings.

Owing to the habit of the artists of introducing large groups of accessory figures and spectators, who are not active participants in the scene represented, and who mainly fill the foreground of the painting, these works frequently lack variety and interest of action. On the other hand, they always offer interesting studies of contemporary Italian costume and individuality. As entire compositions they are very important as illustrating, by contrast, the great advance made after the time of the "Last Supper."

It is in the draping, pose, action, and physiognomy of the individual figures, and in the realistic accessories and background details that we notice their own epoch-making importance in contrast with earlier times. Comparison with contemporary paintings of northern Europe, among which the Flemish and German would offer most accessible illustration, is one good way to appreciate their value. But however remarkable these pictures become in the history of design, when compared with earlier Italian or northern contemporary work, we shall fail of hitting the mark if we consider them purely or mainly from the standpoint of the artist in design.

The main point to be considered is that they represented a public art, existing for the people at large, serving for their education, edification, and instruction. We must bear constantly in mind their individual large dimensions and the fact that all chapels, churches, public halls, and civic buildings were habitually decorated with them. They existed for every one, were accessible to every one and largely took the place in the education of the time, now occupied by printed books. These were just coming into use in the later part of the fifteenth century, but had not yet usurped the place hitherto filled by the pictures.

It is, moreover, to be constantly kept in view that the subjects themselves were traditional and familiar to the thought of the time. Thus they were popular in the best sense. When we consider, finally, the nature of the subjects treated, as regards elevation of thought and wide significance, even apart from their sacred character, the position of Italian painting in the history of culture begins to dawn upon us.

There is, then, this threefold point of view for fifteenth century Italian paintings. First, considering the arts of drawing and painting in their relation to visible nature and in their ability to represent it, as important departments of modern culture, we observe that fifteenth century Italy first acquired and developed this knowledge and that our own knowledge is a traditional inheritance from this period.

Second, considering the general interest of the early Renaissance for modern history, it is a great point that we are able so closely to revive the memories of this time through the medium of pictures which so faithfully portray the facts of its own life, although generally Biblical in subject.

Third, we learn to appreciate the importance of Italian art as a part of the intellectual and educational apparatus of the nation at large, its large patronage for public purposes, and the significance of its subjects as revealing the interests and modes of thought of the common people.

As matter-of-fact history concerning the development of this earliest Renaissance style, we emphasize its wonderfully sudden first appearance in the art of Masaccio; considering that the fourteenth century period, headed by Giotto, did not make any advances beyond the limits he himself had reached and that the dates of Masaccio's pictures in the Brancacci Chapel are the very earliest dates for anything in painting distinct from the style of Giotto.

Although the name of Masolino is generally known as that of Masaccio's teacher, and although his participation in the execution of certain frescoes in this chapel has been asserted by Vasari,* we should, admitting this participation, which is doubted by the great critic, Jacob Burck-

---

* Author of the " Lives of the Artists," written in the sixteenth century.

hardt, still have the same fact to emphasize regarding the
sudden development of the new style, for the paintings by
Masolino near Milan are later than those of the Florentine
Chapel.

As matter-of-fact history, we again emphasize the absence
of any important ad-
vance beyond the style
of Masaccio until the
very close of the fif-
teenth century. Many
of its later artists con-
tinued its traditions
into the sixteenth cen-
tury, in which they
overlap and post-date
the epoch-making
works of that time.

In the fifteenth cen-
tury, as related to the
fourteenth, we can only
quote one similar case
of an overlap of style,
that of the Florentine
artist, Fra Angelico of

Fig. 62.—Detail from the Fresco of " Peter and
Paul Curing the Sick and Lame." Probably
by Masaccio. Brancacci Chapel, Florence.

Fiesole, who in many ways reminds us of the Giotto period.
For piety and simple purity of conception this artist monk
holds a place distinctly his own (Fig. 63).

We have so far made no mention of the altar pieces—the
Madonna pictures, pictures of saints, and Biblical painting
on panel. These were painted for shrines, chapels, and
churches, as devotional pictures. They consequently exhibit a more traditional quality and resemble one another as
types more closely than the wall frescoes, in which con-

temporary secular life was so largely used to convey Biblical subjects. The idea of fifteenth century art derived from these latter pictures would, for this reason, be a narrow one—and yet they are the only pictures which foreign museums or galleries can display, because they are the only ones which are transferable or portable.

We should remember, then, that such paintings represent a minor field of the whole art of the time in spite of their number, interest, and frequent beauty. Their destination for an altar or shrine is to be constantly kept in view, and should not be overlooked because the picture has been transferred to a gallery of paintings. This destination involved serious devotional appearance and was characterized by traditional repetitions of certain set arrangements and motives. As studied in their details these oil paintings will, however, give interesting evi-

FIG. 63.—Detail from the Framing of a Madonna. By Fra Angelico. Uffizi Gallery, Florence.

dence of the realistic tendencies of the age, especially when compared with earlier works.

A point of much importance in the estimate of these panel pictures is that painting in oil colors, then newly introduced from Flanders, where the Van Eycks had first

successfully practiced it, had not yet begun to treat the
lights and shadows, or to represent the figures, with that
soft modelling which Da Vinci was the first to practice
and teach.

In fresco (painting on walls) distinct outlines, without
shading, were the desideratum, because the balance of outlines and figures had to be considered for architectural results.
The oil paintings of this period show us in reality the methods usual in fresco and have consequently a certain hardness

FIG. 64.—Meeting of Mary and Elizabeth.   By Ghirlandajo.   Louvre.

and formalism of outlines which rather obscure their really faithful studies of the human figure and of natural objects.

To this same appearance of formalism was also contributory the very anxiety and painstaking efforts of art to represent that which was actual and real in nature.

As far as the names of the painters are concerned, and aside from those already mentioned, we feel disposed to lay stress on those who were related as teachers and masters to the great artists of the next generation.

Michael Angelo, for instance, had been an apprentice in the studio of Ghirlandajo (frescoes in Maria Novella, Florence) although his most direct predecessor as regards the study of the nude and fore-shortening of the figure was Luca Signorelli (frescoes in Orvieto).

Raphael's master is generally said to have been Perugino, but recent researches of the great Italian critic, Giovanni Morelli, have quite clearly proven that Timoteo della Vite was Raphael's first teacher and that his connection with Perugino was of later date than is usually supposed.

Fig. 65.—Detail from the Series of Paintings by Carpaccio for the Story of St. Ursula. Reception of the English Ambassadors.

Leonardo da Vinci's teacher in painting was Verocchio (Verokyo), who was still more distinguished as a sculptor.

All of these names belong to the Florentine School. The
only great rival school of fifteenth century painting was that
of Padua, headed by Mantegna, whose specialties were
anatomy, perspective, and foreshortening. The effort of
the century to realize nature in art with scientific exactitude
reached its climax in Mantegna as far as painting is concerned. The hardness and formalism then characteristic of
this effort are correspondingly prominent in his work. In
the late fifteenth century we observe the first activity of
Venetian painters under inspirations drawn from the School
of Padua.

Among these earlier Venetians, Carpaccio (Carpatchyo)
stands foremost in interest when the study of the contemporary Italian life is in question. His series of pictures
in the Academy of Venice for the life of Saint Ursula is a
famous authority for costumes and daily life in fifteenth century Venice. The two brothers Bellini of Venice, like
Perugino, lived in both the fifteenth and sixteenth centuries,
and according as earlier or later paintings are selected will
represent the style of one or the other century. The early
art of Giovanni Bellini, the more important of the two
brothers, will serve as an excellent illustration of the hard
effects and painstaking formalism of Mantegna and the
Paduan School, from which he was an offshoot.

CHAPTER XV.

WE MAY leave the fifteenth century style with some remarks regarding the frequency of the Madonna, saints, and Biblical subjects, subsequently to continue.

We occasionally hear complaints from modern travelers as to the limited range of the old Italian subjects and their constant repetitions. Mark Twain's "Innocents Abroad" contains many allusions of this nature, jocose in themselves and well enough in a professedly comic book, but very significant reminders also of remarks otherwise made seriously. This complaint overlooks the point that the fact of repetition was essential to the greatness of Italian art. The repetition of subject argues a popular demand, and this demand

FIG. 66.—Detail of a Madonna by Filippo Lippi. Pitti Palace, Florence.

argues a popular interest. This popular interest is the necessary support of all great art, which cannot exist with-

out it, and which can never become great simply by the
patronage of persons of wealth.   The subject which can be
repeated is the subject which has general interest in the
time which called for it.
More than this, we
assert that the subjects
of Italian art were
worth repeating, and
that the later substi-
tution of literature for
art is our only excuse,
and possibly an insuf-
ficient one, for our own
modern lack of a cor-
responding Biblical art.
The fact of repetition
does not imply any-
thing but an absorption
of the public mind in a
certain range of sub-
jects, for the artist re-
flects his age. Our first
point of view with old
pictures is to ask what

FIG. 67.—Virgin Adoring the Infant Savior.
By Lorenzo di Credi. London.

they teach us about the people for whom they were made.

It may be said next that both with Greek statues and
Italian paintings, the repetition of subjects involved in the
national interest in those subjects is what led to the ultimate
great technical achievements of the men of great genius.
It was also the explanation of the great average perfection
of art during given generations, for average perfection
means, of course, that the artist of ordinary or inferior
capacity did comparatively better than would be naturally

expected. On this last head it is clear that the artist of subordinate talent, working for a demand which repeats the subject, is able to profit by the conceptions of his greater predecessors or contemporaries. In other words, not only the subject but also the treatment is to a large extent traditional.

Originality of conception was not forced upon an artist who did not possess it. It was not even demanded of an artist of genius or of high rank. Raphael's "Betrothal of Mary and Joseph," in Milan, copies closely a picture by Perugino. The pose of the figures on Ghiberti's doors was borrowed by the same painter. The paintings of Leonardo's pupils are with difficulty distinguished from those of the master. Repetition, not only of subject, but also of poses and conceptions, was the rule rather than the exception.

Fig. 68.—The Virgin and Child with two Saints. Perugino. London.

The evolution of scientific design was much assisted by these conditions, as the artist of superior genius started with a fund of ready-made and traditional knowledge for the given subject, to which he was able to add something of his own. The great watchword, "coöperation," was applied, practically,

FIG. 69.—Martyrdom of St. Sebastian.   Pollajuolo.
Pitti Palace, Florence.

in Italian art long be-
fore theorists had
worked out its impor-
tance for social prob-
lems. We may point
this moral by allusion
to the St. Sebastian
subject. This was for
nearly two centuries
the one type in which
the nude form was con-
stantly studied (Fig.
69).

We must not forget
that both with the
Greeks and the Ital-
ians the repetition of
subject means that art
existed to represent and
teach belief—in other
words, it means that
art was religious.

The first and main
advantage of Italian
painting over all which
has followed was that
the subject-matter itself
was superior in im-
portance to any which
the art of painting has
since handled. It was
Christian art in the best
and highest sense, and

in such a sense that all beliefs and all sects of our own time unite in proclaiming its greatness. Just as we may, and do, in a strictly literary sense, consider the Bible as great and classic literature because its style is a living reflex of its noble and inspired teaching, so may the Italian art of the early sixteenth century be viewed as a translation of the Bible into the language of forms, fully worthy of the great original. The story of Genesis was told on the ceiling of the Sistine Chapel in a way which revived the old Hebrew simplicity and grandeur of Genesis itself. The lives of the Apostles live again in the cartoons and tapestries of Raphael, and the treachery of Judas has gone down to history in the great fresco of Da Vinci, as well as in the translation of King James the First, or the Revised Version.

That only a highly refined and cultivated general taste and a generally high level of civilization could account for the great pictures of the sixteenth century is also apparent, after slender knowledge of them. Whether we come to the knowledge of this civilization first through the picture, as many of us do, or whether we come to the picture through a knowledge of the civilization, as some few of us do— makes little difference. Each helps to explain and illustrate the other.

We shall, then, at the outset abandon the idea that we are dealing with a phenomenal existence of some five or six "Old Masters," who happened fortuitously and by some strange accident to have been born within the limits of one generation some four hundred years ago. We shall rather consider these few artists as only the tallest among many other giants—the waves which rise a little higher than the ocean of their fellows.

The average excellence of Italian painting between 1500 and 1530 is a much more remarkable fact than the existence of its first-quoted and much-quoted phenomenal geniuses.

This average excellence is one phase and one illustration of a perfection of civilization and of that high degree of material prosperity in the most modern sense, which I have previously endeavored to describe in matter introductory to the architecture of the Renaissance and tending to explain its subsequent diffusion and still continuing traditional power.

We have already seen that the "Last Supper," of Leonardo da Vinci (Vinchy) in Milan, fixes the high-water mark of Italian painting after which the tide stood at its full till 1530. To comprehend the incredible industry, activity, and ambition of the Italian painters in the intervening time, we must remember the great patronage devoted to their art, the great wealth of the cities, princes, popes, and prelates whom they served, the stirring life and stirring rivalries of these small Italian States in which, for the time being, all the vigor of later modern civilization was bottled and confined.

Industries and pursuits were not specialized, as in later times; the great painters were generally sculptors, architects, and engineers in the bargain. Many others were jewelers and designers in metal. The architect Brunellesco was a competitor for the commission of designing the first set of bronze doors for the Florence Baptistery which were done by Ghiberti, and otherwise ranked as one of the leading sculptors of his day. The architect Michelozzo was the greatest bronze-caster of his time, and actually cast the famous bronze doors designed by Ghiberti. Fra Giocondo, who, after Bramante, was for some time employed on St. Peter's Church, is thought, by Jacob Burckhardt, to have been the greatest architect of his day, but he figures in Vasari's "Lives" especially as a painter, and the most interesting story told of his life concerns his talent in nursery gardening. He was also a civil engineer, and a man of letters of such distinction that we owe to him the discovery, in the Library at Paris, of the Letters of Pliny. It was this same Fra Giocondo who first published in print the announcement of the discovery of the New World.* Michael Angelo was poet, engineer, military general, politician, architect, sculptor, and painter. Leonardo da Vinci was an improvising poet, a musician who was able also to make his own instruments, an athlete, an anatomist, an author, a civil and military engineer, an expert in the construction of canals, as well as architect, sculptor, and painter. His accomplishments included also a knowledge of botany, mathematics, and astronomy. He is the first modern by whom hints for the later science of geology were given.

---

* Fiske's " Discovery of America "—the other facts in Vasari.

CHAPTER XVI.

LEONARDO DA VINCI.

To say that Leonardo da Vinci was foremost in time and the equal of any sixteenth century painter, is to say that he was the greatest, for this was a period when no new artist failed to profit by everything which had been done up to date.

This artist was born near Florence in the middle of the fifteenth century (1452). We must therefore concede that he had reached the maturity of his powers long before the opening of the sixteenth century. We cannot, however, point to any decisive revolution in fifteenth century style, owing to his influence or otherwise, before the close of the century. This may be attributed mainly to the very small number of paintings produced by him before the time of the "Last Supper." This again would be explained by his versatility of pursuits and occupations as above

FIG. 70.—Portrait of Leonardo da Vinci. (Doubtfully ascribed to himself as artist.) Uffizi Gallery, Florence.

described, and also by his long and arduous devotion to self-training by technical experiments and technical studies, as distinct from an activity devoted to the production of completed paintings for sale and public inspection.

At present perhaps a dozen pictures or less would cover the number definitely known as his. The wonderful quality of these becomes still more wonderful when we compare the contemporary and just preceding work. Hard and distinct outline had been the rule alike for fresco and oil painting. Da Vinci was the first to differentiate these arts and to distinguish between the decorative and architectural conditions of the wall-painting, and the possibilities of illusion in oil painting attainable by the use of lights and

FIG. 71.—" La Gioconda." Portrait by Da Vinci, Louvre.

shadows. He was the first to perceive that forms in nature are rarely seen in hard outlines, but rather in masses of color, and to realize that insistance on the outline in painting must be at the expense of realistic illusion, for we thus become aware that the background is a surface and not a background. In architectural painting it is desirable, however, that the background should appear as a surface; nor

did Da Vinci or his followers depart from this point of
view in wall-painting, although he employed oil color for
the "Last Supper." In panel painting, his great art in the
modeling of the figure was, however, to present it as
merging into the background, and yet as projected from it.
The sense of mystery inspired by his handling has such
effect on the imagination that we cease to say to ourselves:
"This is only a picture." The picture itself becomes a
mysterious reality, something to be considered and thought
over, gradually coming nearer to us as we consider it, or re-

FIG. 72.—The Virgin and St. Anne. Da Vinci.
Louvre.

ceding as we abandon
serious contemplation
of it. It is, in fact,
itself a creation of in-
tellect and of thought.

His most famous oil
painting is the portrait
of a lady in the Louvre,
known as "La Gio-
conda," a still world-
famous picture, which
was purchased for a
large sum by the
French king, Francis
I., during the lifetime
of the artist.

In this painting and
in the picture of the
Virgin and St. Anne

in the same Collection, we find a mastery of light and
shadow and of modeling which our earlier illustrations of
Italian painting have not revealed. The shadows of his
pictures as darkened by time, make them, however, diffi-

cult subjects for photograph. In oil painting, Da Vinci was undoubtedly the first modern artist who reached complete success.

The type of face which he affected in female subjects has a refined and subtle character. In the "Gioconda" we find it difficult, for instance, to decide whether or no the face be smiling. As regards the number of oil paintings positively ascribed to him, the march of criticism in recent years has more and more tended to reverse previous attributions and assign works to his scholars which bear his name. This is at least a credit to the capacities of his pupils and to his profound influence on Italian painting.

Da Vinci's epoch-making work was the "Last Supper," painted on the wall of the Refectory of the Convent of Santa Maria delle Grazie, in Milan; and no other wall-painting now remains from his hand.*

In the year following its completion (or to be assumed as year of completion, for we only know positively that it was finished before 1499), the artist was driven from Milan by the French invasion, which overthrew the rule of the duke who was his patron and protector. His subsequent career was much disturbed by the complications of Italian politics, and his last years were spent in France, under the protection of the king, Francis I., whose personal friendship he enjoyed. He died at Amboise in 1519.

In the "Last Supper," Italian painting reached its climax. Although much damaged by flaking off, by repainting of the faces, and other injuries (a door, for instance, was broken through the wall beneath), the picture still has an indescribable effect of mysterious power over the spectator. This is attributable, in the first in-

---

* The fresco in the Convent of San Onofrio, at Rome, is now ascribed to Beltraffio.

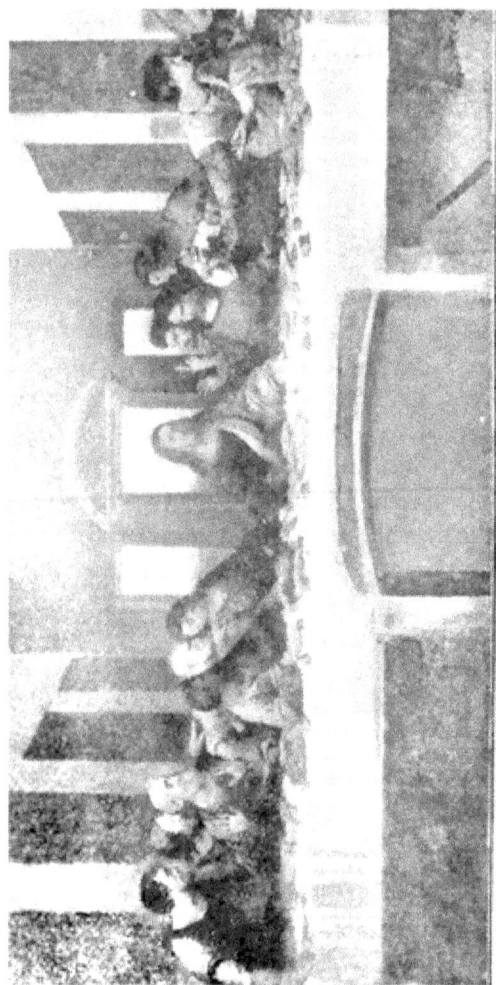

FIG. 73.—The "Last Supper." Da Vinci. Milan.

stance, to its dimensions; the individual figures being nearly double life-size. The fine harmony of color, dramatic power, and psychologic insight into character displayed by varied gesture and expression, the way in which the action cumulates toward the figure of the Savior, the dispersion into groups, each with its own distinct story, are some of the elements contributing to this effect. Nor should we underrate the influence of the subject itself. There is no moment in the story of the Passion of such far-reaching significance, and its portrayal was a fitting subject for the crowning effort of Italian art.

' All engravings of this painting fail to suggest its power by virtue of a certain flatness in the outlined effect. In the photograph we realize more clearly the varieties of plane in the grouping of the apostles. Finally, it is apparent, in this picture above all others, how a profound knowledge of human nature must underlie the talent of the hand and eye when a great work of art is in question.

It will most easily define the relations of later Italian painting to Da Vinci, to specify the ages of the great contemporary artists when this work was finished. Raphael, for instance, was only fifteen years of age and Correggio was but four years old. Michael Angelo was twenty-three years old, Titian was twenty-one years old.

Knowing, as we do, the active rivalry at this time of the Italian artists and their eagerness to learn from one another, it would be clear, simply from this comparison of dates, what Leonardo's influence must have been. His competition with Michael Angelo five years later for a commission to decorate the Municipal Palace of Florence, shows the rapidity with which the younger artists were pushing forward. The cartoon drawings made for this competition were never executed and were subsequently destroyed.

All that is known of them is by the engravings from
fragments known as the "Battle of the Standard" by Da
Vinci and the "Bathing Soldiers" by Michael Angelo.

FIG. 74.—Fresco by Luini at Lugano. The Virgin,
Infant Jesus, and Infant John.

To the influence of these cartoons on contemporary art,
about and after 1504, is ascribed the final flower of Italian
painting.

The personal pupils and followers of Leonardo must be
distinguished from the mass of Italian painters, who were
ultimately and more indirectly influenced by him.   Among
the former, Luini is the most distinguished in general
reputation as regards close connection with Da Vinci, but
the influence of Fra Bartolommeo of Florence was more
distinctly powerful as mediating between the great painter
and the artists of a contemporaneous but younger generation.   On Raphael the influence of Fra Bartolommeo is especially apparent and very generally recognized.

CHAPTER XVII.

RAPHAEL SANTI OF URBINO.

THERE are certain reasons for making a central figure of this artist in a brief account of the zenith of Italian painting, aside from his undeniable distinction as a painter, and without prejudice to the distinction of his great contemporaries.

Raphael was much more prolific in the production of pictures than Da Vinci, more intellectual and more monumental in his art than Titian or Correggio, and in the duration of his life and in his style more strictly confined to the greatest period of Italian art than Michael Angelo. It was the fate of the latter to live into the time of the decadence, and in some ways to influence and determine its character.

FIG. 75.—House in Urbino where Raphael was born.

It will be worth while here, for a moment, to turn back to the illustration of the palace built for the dukes of Urbino, as reminder of the existence of the state which was Raphael's home (Fig. 35).

Two facts in the history of the little state of Urbino are significant for the relation of Raphael to general Italian history. One is that its library, as subsequently united with the library of the Vatican, was the most important addition ever made to the latter, and the library of the Vatican is the most important historic library of the world. A state whose dukes were thus fond of books was naturally fitted to be an important center of Italian culture. What this importance was may now be argued from a curious fact in the history of the popes.

Fig. 76.—The Camera della Segnatura in the Vatican as decorated by Raphael, and showing a Portion of the "Philosophy or "School of Athens."

In the history of the Renaissance the court of Pope Leo X. (1513-1521) is generally held up to admiration as the center of art and learning, as the culmination of the glories of the Renaissance. It is not so generally understood that the artists and men of learning who surrounded Leo X. were mainly inherited by him from the preceding pope, Julius II., who was the first great patron of Bramante, of Michael Angelo, and of Raphael; the projector of the

Sistine Chapel and Vatican frescoes, of the Raphael cartoons, and of St. Peter's Church. Now Julius II. belonged to the family of Rovere, which was connected by
marriage with the family of the dukes of Urbino. It was
from the connections and associates of the court of Urbino
that he drew together the circle of great men, which ultimately made the reputation of the court of Leo X.

This fact has a double significance. It illustrates the intellectual atmosphere which influenced Raphael's boyhood.

His own father was
court poet as well as
court painter. It also
explains how the trans-
fer of Raphael's activ-
ity to Rome, in 1508,
made when he was
only twenty-five years
old, placed him among
acquaintances to whom
he was already favor-
ably known.

In this center of in-
tellectual and personal
refinement Raphael's
engaging personality
and kindly nature
combined with his un-
tiring industry, great

FIG. 77.—Plato and Aristotle. From the " School
of Athens." Vatican. By Raphael.

talents, and rapidly acquired fame to make him a leading
figure.

Both in the methods and subjects of his art he was destined to become the representative painter of the classic
and literary enthusiasms of the Renaissance. These found

their culmination in his great wall-paintings in the Vatican
known as "Philosophy," or "The School of Athens";
"Poetry," or "The Parnassus"; "Jurisprudence"; and
"Theology." All the knowledge that the science of design in Italy had mastered in ten years following the completion of the "Last Supper" was also at his command.

To this hard-earned knowledge, first won by other artists, was added his own distinguished talent as painter and draughtsman and a peculiar tact in the arrangement, balance, and spacing, of his compositions.

As a composer of designs in and for architectural surrounding and on architectural surfaces, Raphael stands without a rival

FIG. 78.—Apollo. Detail of the "Parnassus" by Raphael. Vatican.

in modern art. In Michael Angelo we admire the volcanic genius, the colossal power; in Raphael we find a
calmer, better balanced, and, so to speak, more architectural spirit.

It is, then, in the relation of outlines to surrounding
space and framing that his distinctive mastery lies. This
most conspicuous quality of his oil paintings reflects his
architectural training and architectural point of view. To
this was added a perception for pure and spiritual beauty in

women and in children, and for noble dignity in men. All
these qualities are revealed in that room of the Vatican, the
Camera della Segnatura ("Room of the Signature," that
is to say, the pope's office) which he began to decorate in
1508 with the frescoes whose subjects have been named
above.

At a later date Raphael executed the ten monumental
designs for tapestry pictures of the Lives of the Apostles

FIG. 79.—Detail from the "Jurisprudence." By Raphael. Vatican.

whose cartoons (as far as preserved) are now in the South
Kensington Museum of London, while the tapestries them-
selves are preserved in duplicate sets in Berlin and in the
Vatican (the latter formerly in the Sistine Chapel).

Between the dates of these two monumental sets of works

he executed the fresco decoration of several Vatican rooms adjoining the Camera della Segnatura, and a series of over fifty designs from Old Testament history known as " Raphael's Bible." These last were executed by scholars on the ceiling of the Vatican corridor designed by Bramante, and known as the " Loggie" (lodgeay) of Raphael (Fig. 58).

FIG. 80.—Detail of the "Madonna in the Meadow." By Raphael. Vienna.

To this catalogue of untiring activity we must now add the frescoes from classic subjects (the story of Cupid and Psyche) executed by scholars on the ceiling of the Farnesina Villa and an enormous number of oil paintings; Madonnas, Biblical subjects, and portraits.

Of his Madonnas the " Sistine," in Dresden, is the largest, most imposing, and most famous. Of his other oil paintings the "Transfiguration" of the Vatican Gallery is the most celebrated.

His portraits are marvels of character portrayal and a perpetual monument to the intellectual refinement and cultivation of his time. Here, as elsewhere, the quality of his painting has a peculiar solidity and strength combined with refinement of finish. When we consider the enormous amount and the even quality of his personal work (as distinct from that of some frescoes on which scholars were employed) he appears as a miracle of industry as well as of art.

We have already quoted Raphael's activity as the architect of several palaces in Rome and Florence and as successor of Bramante in the construction of St. Peter's. As a

FIG. 81.—Detail from the "Betrothal of Mary and Joseph."
By Raphael. Milan.

sculptor, we are able to mention at least two statues from his models, the "Jonah" in Rome and the "Cupid with the Dolphin" in St. Petersburg.

One of my illustrations has been chosen to show Raphael's early relations to fifteenth century art (Fig. 81). The "Betrothal of Mary and Joseph" is closely copied from a Perugino now at Caen, in northern France. The

faces of Perugino's paintings (Fig. 68) are constantly
repeated in Raphael's early pictures. I do not bring this
up as a fact remarkable in itself, but as illustrating what I
have already said regarding coöperation, tradition, and the
repetition of subjects in Italian art (p. 127). This picture
is also interesting as illustrating (in a small oil painting)
the style of composition and arrangement of figures common to most frescoes of the fifteenth century. It would
serve, in fact, as an
excellent type of illus-
tration for that period
of fresco.

FIG. 82.—Detail of the Portrait of Angiolo Doni.
By Raphael. Pitti Palace.

I am inclined to add
a word regarding the
point in which Raphael
must be considered as
the superior of all later
moderns who have so
far attempted similar
monumental deco-
rations. The number
of these is not large,
and in all modern art
Kaulbach's frescoes on
the walls of the great
staircase of the Berlin
Museum are probably
the nearest approach to a similar scale and class of subjects.

Although Raphael's period was one of great proficiency
in drawing, of refinement in the harmonious use of colors,
and of a quick and spontaneous interest in seizing the
active motion of the body in moments and poses having
both dignity and beauty when arrested perpetually by

art—we cannot say that science in design is alone the
secret of its success. Were this the case, it would be hard
to understand why a modern as conscientious and as pro-
ficient as Kaulbach
should take a lower
rank. We must real-
ize, as one element of
superiority, the habit
of off-hand, bold, and
rapid work cultivated
by the art of painting
on plaster. Our mod-
ern art is not offered
sufficient practice in
wall decoration, and in
life-size figure compo-
sition, to cultivate in
the artist the same
security and self-confi-
dence in his own re-
sources. He may by
a great exertion of care
and personal effort
reach a comparable
stage of perfection in

FIG. 83.—Portrait of Maddalena Doni. By
Raphael. Pitti Palace, Florence.

his science, but he will have sacrificed in the very labor-
iousness of his effort the dash and spirit, the off-hand freedom of the old design. The key to the effect of a large
work of art lies in a relation of the parts to the whole,
in which an over-careful finish of details has not destroyed
the effect of concentration, the power of the leading
thought. Elaboration of detail is suited to a small oil
painting, but not to a large one—certainly not to a wall-

painting.   Far apart as is the art of the modern Japanese
and the Italian art, the former offers the best parallel when
the suggestiveness of an effect as attained by a limitation of
detail is in question.   The photograph details of Raphael's
frescoes (shown in this chapter) will give valuable hints on
this point.

We may again suggest that the dignity, reserve, and

nobility of Raphael's
art are attainable only
when the artist is work-
ing for a public which
is certain to appreciate
his effort, because its
own best thoughts and
noblest ideas have been
translated for it into
form.   In this element
of perfection we come
back to the point of
view that the greatest
art does not represent
simply the thought of
the artist, but that it
must also represent the
overflow and the reflex
of the best thought of

Fig. 84.—Detail of the "Transfiguration" by
Raphael. Vatican Gallery.

the age to which he belongs.   The nineteenth century
more generally expects from the poet, the man of letters,
and the musical composer, what the Italian Renaissance
asked from the artist in design.

Raphael died in 1520, at the age of thirty-seven.   He
was born in 1483—the birth-year of Luther.   The most
recent and exhaustive history of the artist's life is by

Muntz. The work of Passavant, though written earlier in
our century, is still valuable. The life by Vasari ("Lives
of the Artists") is short and readable, giving practically all
that is known of the person and social life of the artist.
Vasari's book was written about the middle of the sixteenth
century, and is the main original authority for the lives of all
the Italian painters who lived before that time. Although
in matters of criticism, and in matters of detail, it is occasionally open to correction and revision, the fact that its
writer lived in the same period with the subjects of his interesting sketches, gives his book unique worth. The English
translation (Bohn Edition) successfully follows the quaint
style of the original.

CHAPTER XVIII.

MICHAEL ANGELO BUONARROTI.

WHERE the element of character and personality is so largely involved in our estimate of an artist's work, as it is with this painter, we should do well to bear in mind the importance of his statues (see forward) as assisting us to comprehend and place him. Michael Angelo's position as a painter is fixed solely by his works in the Sistine Chapel. His few panel pictures, three or four in number, are not much more than interesting curiosities, when large facts are in question.

FIG. 85.—Bust of Michael Angelo, dating 1570. From his Tomb in Church of Santa Croce, Florence. By Battista Lorenzi.

In this Chapel, where his great triumph as a painter was celebrated, we must first distinguish between the "Last Judgment," painted late in life on its end wall, and the much earlier ceiling frescoes for the "Story of Genesis," with the attendant decorative compositions.

The whole Chapel with its earlier fifteenth century frescoes
on the side walls, below which were once hung the tapestries of Raphael, is a fine reminder of the ideals of the

Fig. 86.—Creation of the Sun and Moon. Detail from the Ceiling of
the Sistine Chapel.

Renaissance in the matter of interior decoration. This
apartment, which still serves as the papal chapel of the
Vatican, has its name from the pope, Sixtus IV., who
built it about 1473.

Michael Angelo's original profession was that of sculptor,
and as such he had already won his reputation before the
ceiling pictures were begun (in 1508). His "David" in
Florence had just been completed; his "Bacchus" and
"Pietà" are also earlier works. In this profession he was
already remarkable for colossal and grandiose conceptions,
and the tomb of Julius II., which was to have been the

central feature of St. Peter's Church, was already one of
his commissions. Even in the later and diminished proportions of this tomb, as placed in another Roman church, the
statue of "Moses" is still the most imposing piece of
modern statuary, while the "Captives" of the Louvre,
which were detached from the tomb after the changes in its
plans, made after the death of the pope, are counterparts
in importance of his Tombs of the Medici, subsequently
done in Florence.

In these various works of sculpture an imperious and
daring genius of conception is supported by profound

FIG. 87.—Detail from the Series representing the Forefathers of Christ.
Sistine Chapel Ceiling.

knowledge of the anatomy of the human figure, and by a
wonderful technical ability in the use of the chisel. But in
sculpture Michael Angelo expressed his own great person-

ality. In the ceiling frescoes of the Sistine Chapel, this personality became the servant of Christian art in such a way that the greatness of the man united with the greatness of his time and of his subject to produce a most wonderful work of Bible illustration.

To tell the story of the Creation in pictures worthily and grandly, is a task which no other artist of any period has accomplished. Even the mere physical execution of a work of such vast extent was a miracle of personal fortitude and endurance. To calculate, while lying on his back on a scaffold close to the ceiling, the proper proportions of detail treatment for effect on the distant floor below, was one of the least of his tasks.

Among these subjects of the ceiling the "Creation of the Sun and Moon," the "Creation of Adam," the "Creation of Eve," the "Temptation and Expulsion from the Garden of Eden," are the most remarkable.

In the angular recesses of the vaulting and in the arched spaces above the windows were represented the "Forefathers of Christ." The ruling thought of these compositions is to illustrate the expectant transition stage of history waiting for the new dispensation of Christ.

Between the triangular recesses of the ceiling are arranged the "Prophets" and "Sibyls," representing Hebrew and pagan inspiration according to an Italian artistic method which conceived of inspired thought as common to the classic and the Jewish literature.

The panels of the main ceiling, devoted to the "Story of Genesis," are alternately wide and narrow. At the angles thus formed between the panels are placed the nude male figures commonly called personifications of architectural force. There can be no question but that these various frescoes, when viewed in their combination and vast ex-

FIG. 88.—The Sistine Chapel. Vatican Palace.

tent, are the most daring and successful effort of architectural decoration ever undertaken by man.

Twenty-two years after the completion of the ceiling frescoes (finished 1512) the "Last Judgment" on the rear wall of the chapel was begun. Its enormous dimensions, sixty feet in height, and bold designs will always extort the admiration of the beholder. At the same time we must confess to a certain coldness of appreciation for this work by contrast with our feeling for the "Story of Genesis." As far as this lies in the failure of the picture to correspond to the imaginative demand made upon it, we must remember that such a failure must be involved in any picture of the subject, and this would have been conceded instantly by the artist and by his time.

We will begin our estimate of the "Last Judgment" by acknowledging that this subject, which we could not imagine a nineteenth century painter as even attempting, had its proper place in art when the mission of art was to illustrate Bible literature and to represent Christian belief. Therefore, instead of approaching the "Last Judgment" from the standpoint of the nineteenth century, which is really that of imaginative literature, we must approach it from the standpoint of the sixteenth century, which is that of imaginative painting. But when the picture is viewed from the standpoint of its own period, as one more treatment of a traditional religious subject which was inside the limits of art because the whole Middle Age, and the early Renaissance as well, had represented its religious ideals, beliefs, and teachings by means of art, we must still admit some shortcomings in the "Last Judgment" as compared with other religious art of the time, for instance, as compared with other works by the same man in the same place.

If we should attempt in one sentence to fix this short-

coming, it would be by saying that the studies of the
anatomist and the zeal of the student in fore-shortened
figures have been carried to a point where we lose sight
of the subject in admiring the science of the painter.
It was the greatest virtue of the great time that its technical
science in details did not overpower its idea, and that the
whole was always greater than its parts, even when taken

Fig. 89.—Detail from the " Last Judgment" by Michael Angelo.
Angels with the Pillar of Christ's Scourging.

together.   In the " Last Judgment " the parts taken
separately or together are perhaps more admirable than
the whole.

This much having been said in qualification, as against
an unconditionally enthusiastic attitude toward this great
picture, we are forced to admit that it is the largest and

in many senses the most imposing, as it is the latest, of the monumental works of Italian art (the decorations of the Doge's Palace at Venice alone excepted). As an astounding exhibition of power and science in drawing it is undoubtedly, when dimensions and number of figures are considered, the superior of any other single work in the whole world and in that sense the worthy climax in painting of the sculptor of the "Moses," and the architect of St. Peter's dome.

It was the mission of Michael Angelo to astound humanity by a character in which profound scientific and technical knowledge were combined with capacity for enthusiasm and with exalted imaginative power. It has thus been his strange fate to have been admired by two distinct classes of experts—those who lay stress on purely technical science of execution in design without reference to the thought it may have to convey, and those who are captivated by

FIG. 90.—Decorative Figure from the Sistine Chapel Ceiling.

grandeur of thought without reference to the science of execution. As the besetting sin of Italian art in its later decadence was to lay undue stress on technique, without reference to thought and conception, it was possible for

Michael Angelo to satisfy the taste of that period and even
to serve as the model of many of its imitative efforts.   On
the other hand, the most authoritative critics of our own
time class him as a man of mind with Shakespeare and
with the most exalted geniuses of all history in music and
in literature.   .

   Considered as a painter pure and simple, Michael Angelo's forte was the study of the human figure, both in its
anatomic form and in its action as represented by the art of
foreshortening.   As a colorist he does not take high rank,
but it cannot be said that the quality of his art would have
been improved by a different scheme of color.   Where
design considered as drawing is the force of the artist, color
must of necessity be subordinated to this force.   For design emphasizes the outline, while color emphasizes the
surface and the mass.   It must further be said that there is
no other artist whose work so absolutely requires a knowledge of the personality and life as connected with the
history and political revolutions of his time.   Grimm's
"Life of Michael Angelo" treats of these matters in a
most satisfactory way.   Vasari was personally acquainted
with Michael Angelo, and the life written by him is one of
his best, being full of interesting anecdotes and personal
details.

CHAPTER XIX.

DURING the same time when Raphael was enchanting the world with his dignified balance of beautifully varied figures and while Michael Angelo was astounding it with his prodigious illustrations of the old Hebrew literature, another great painter was demonstrating that every kind of talent was contained in this one epoch by a class of pictures which charm and delight us without appealing either to the intellect or to the standpoint of architectural effect.

FIG. 91.—Detail from Correggio's "Virgin Adoring the Infant Savior." Uffizi Gallery, Florence.

Antonio Allegri, known as Correggio (Corejyo), from his birthplace near Parma, was this painter. Correggio was, after Da Vinci, the first great master in lights and shadows. His subjects are as often mytho- logical as religious, and in both cases attractive by grace and beauty rather than by power of thought. He was an artist of the senses

FIG. 92.—Christ Appears to Mary Magdalen after the Resurrection.
Correggio. Madrid.

rather than of the intellect, an oil painter rather than a monumental decorator, rarely dignified but never commonplace.

In Correggio's art the momentary effect in face and gesture was the thing sought for, but this effort never descended to affectation and never sinned by self-consciousness. The greatest charm of Correggio's painting is its artless and innocent delight in sensuous beauty which never sinks to sensuality.

My illustrations for this artist will probably place him in his relations and contrasts to the great Florentines more successfully than words. His tendencies as pursued by a later generation with less simplicity had marked influence on the seventeenth century and all later art. His important pictures, as being oil paintings on canvas, have been widely scattered through the galleries of Europe, all of which can boast one or more of his masterpieces. His "Holy Night" in Dresden, is the most generally known. The "Magdalen" in Dresden, so long attributed to him, is now known to be by Van der Werff, an artist of the seventeenth century school of Holland.

In face of his picture in Madrid of the meeting of Christ and Mary Magdalen after the Resurrection, we cannot deny that Correggio had his serious moments and great thoughts. This is probably his greatest, certainly his most serious, work. The wonderful mellowness of coloring and dark richness of the shadows are seen even in the photograph.

In the execution of minor details Correggio showed the same broad style of execution otherwise familiar to his time but he went much farther in the realistic introduction and treatment of clouds, landscape accessories, and other subordinate features of his pictures. It would be more correct and more exact to say that he habitually represented

these things in larger dimensions as compared with his
figure scheme, than did other contemporary painters.
Altogether his art is more mobile, more expressive in the
exterior sense, more vibratory in its relations of light

Fig. 93.—Hall of the Grand Council, Doge's Palace.

and shade, more nervous in its activity, in a word, more
modern than that of any of his contemporaries.   He is a
marvelous anticipator of the effects which were sought by
all artists a century later, but which were then sought without the same unaffected and ingenuous style.

   We have still left for mention the School of the Venetians,
which outlived all other great art in Italy and continued
in bloom down to the close of the sixteenth century.   The
relations of this survival to general Italian history have

been pointed out (p. 36). As contrasted with the light and shadow treatment of Correggio, the figure design of Michael Angelo, or the decorative composition of Raphael, the great excellence of Venetian painting was its harmony and warmth of color.

Why the Venetians should have been so pre-eminent in color is not immediately clear. We may suggest that their commerce with the East and traffic in Oriental rugs and fabrics may have had much to do with it. Certainly we can find analogies between the warm tones of their pictures and their prosperous, luxurious lives and pleasure-loving tastes.

Oil colors and canvas surface were their preference for interiors as against fresco painting on plaster. Their wall-paintings were canvases fastened to the walls after the work was done. There is not therefore in Venetian art any question of the outline effects and architectural balance of Raphael and other Florentines or of the anatomic enthusiasms of Michael Angelo. On the other hand the contrasts and harmonies of flesh color and draperies, the rich mellowness of backgrounds and skies are absolutely unrivaled either in contemporary or later times.

Fig. 94.—Detail from Titian's Portrait of "La Bella." Pitti Palace, Florence.

FIG. 95.—Detail from Titian's "Assumption of the Virgin." Venice Academy.

To such an art strong emotion or rapid action was generally foreign.   Half-figure pieces were much affected and
here make their appearance for the first time in Italian
art.   (In the seventeenth century they became general.)
A noble and dignified repose is a constant feature of these
paintings.   Nowhere is the great refinement of Italian culture more apparent than in these faces and attitudes.   The
poise and self-contained character of the portraits have been

FIG. 96.—St. Bridget offering Flowers to the Infant Savior. Titian. Madrid.

rarely if ever equaled in later times, and when they are
taken in bulk have never been subsequently rivaled.
What we admire later in Velasquez or in Van Dyck was the
everyday art of a sixteenth century Venetian portrait.

The development of Venetian art was tardy.   Not till
the close of the fifteenth century does it figure, unless in
the studies of the specialist.   We have devoted a word

to Carpaccio and the Bellinis for this time (p. 124).

At the opening of the sixteenth century we are then con-
fronted by a genius in Giorgione (Jorjony), in whom
all the best qualities of Venetian art found their highest

Fig. 97.—Detail from Titian's "Presentation of the Virgin." Venice Academy.

pitch of perfection. To this perfection is added a touch of
aristocratic reticence and refinement which even in Venetian
art has scarcely had its parallel. The paintings of this
artist who died at the age of thirty-four (1511), are of
extreme rarity. The greatest painter of Venetian art beside and after him was his pupil.

To Titian (Tishyan) this place is awarded not because
Palma Vecchio, or Paris Bordone, Tintoretto, or Paul
Veronese, has not rivaled him in many pictures, but

Fig. 98.—Portrait by Palma Vecchio. Vienna.

because his constant evenness of perfection through a
long life of enormous industry and productivity has left
him without a rival when his works are summed together.
The Dresden Gallery will take the palm for Titians in
northern Europe.   In Italy, outside of Venice, his finest
paintings are in Florence and in the Borghese Gallery
at Rome.   His greatest picture is the "Assumption of the
Virgin," in the Venice Academy.   "Christ and the Trib-
ute Money," in Dresden, is his greatest work in northern
Europe.

The nearest rivals of Titian were Palma Vecchio and
Paris Bordone.   The quality of their art is closely analogous
to his.   In amount of production or in thoughtful conceptions of subject matter they cannot be said to have been his

FIG. 99.—Detail from the "Feast in the House of Levi."   By Paul Veronese.
Venice Academy.

equals. For pure Venetian coloring they cannot be called inferiors.

On the other hand Tintoretto and Paul Veronese represent a later generation of Venetian art, in which the solidity and body of the design were tending to become weaker. Only in individual examples does Tintoretto rise to the heights of his predecessors.

Paul Veronese, who closes in point of time the list of great Venetians, was in brush work and in color one of the greatest, but it would be difficult to quote works from his hand of ideal and intellectual quality such as were produced by Giorgione, Titian, and contemporaries. The colossal canvases on which he depicted the "Feast in the House of Levi," the "Marriage of Cana," etc., are purely pictures of Venetian life disguised by their titles as scripture subjects, and we are bound to confess that what had once been the means to an end had now become the end itself.

It is best, however, not to be looking either backward or forward when we wish to be just to a work of art and give it full value for its own sake. He who wishes to do full justice to Veronese needs only to ask himself the question, "How can I best know the daily life of the most opulent and cultivated city of Europe in the days of Shakespeare and Elizabeth?"

We cannot close our brief account of the greatest Italian painters without noting the multitude of artists of the first rank flourishing in the same period, whose names have not been mentioned. A mere catalogue of their names would scarcely be worth making, and space would not allow more. None the less their existence, at least, must be specified and insisted on. It is this multitude of superior artists which made possible the supreme perfection of the work of certain individuals of rarest genius among their number.

CHAPTER XX.

SEVENTEENTH CENTURY RENAISSANCE PAINTING.

To FIND the Renaissance art of the seventeenth century at its best we must turn first to Spain or the Netherlands, where the works of Velasquez and Murillo, Rubens, Van Dyck and Rembrandt continued in original ways and with some distinct national qualities the traditions of their Italian predecessors. For the general spread of Italian culture over northern Europe, which carried the Italian arts of design in its train, see my matter on the general history and architecture of the Renaissance.

FIG. 100.—Portrait of Henrietta of France, Queen of Charles I. of England. Van Dyck. Pitti Palace, Florence.

The art of painting now becomes an art like other arts, no longer destined to bear on its shoulders the whole spiritual thought and mission of an epoch or to raise to the highest pitch the monumental effect of magnificent buildings; but in a more limited sphere, as the art still

exists for ourselves, a noble continuation and development
of the lessons of the earlier great masters.

The changed position of the art of painting is to be
ascribed ultimately to the introduction of printed books,
to the new methods of education and expression which were
consequently less dependent on the language of forms, and
to · an enlargement of national boundaries in which the
direct relation of the artist to an entire civic community
as the banner-bearer of its pride and ambitions was necessarily abandoned.

Perhaps we may add that as the study of nature and the
science of form had been the great triumph of Italy over

FIG. 101.—The Dead Savior in the Lap of the Virgin. Van Dyck. Antwerp.

the Middle Age, it was natural that this triumph should
have been announced and celebrated most enthusiastically
when it was first won.

The use of books affected Catholic as well as Protestant countries, but in the former, religious pictorial subjects
were traditional and were not abandoned, whereas in the

latter they were for the time being formally offensive to the
religious standpoint of the day.   These religious subjects, as
found in Catholic countries, were continued, however, on a
much diminished scale of magnitude and number.   The
wall decoration of churches was practically abandoned.   Not

FIG. 102.—"Jacob's Ladder."   Ribera.   Madrid.

much, at least, worth quoting was done in this line.   Nor
could the Catholic artists avoid reflecting the tendency of
their time in which the representation of visible nature for
its own sake had begun to be the main thing.   A closer
illusion as regards momentary reality, the imitation of
fabrics or of trappings, was now generally in vogue in religious art.   In expression the sentimental rather than the
dignified was commonly sought.

If therefore we wish to place the time as a whole, we must

remember that Shakespeare was still writing his later plays
(died 1616), that Cervantes and Calderon produced in
it the great masterpieces of Spanish literature, that Cor-

FIG. 103.—Portrait of the Dwarf El Primo. Velasquez. Madrid.

neille and Molière, during its lapse, raised the French
drama to its pinnacle of glory. The age of Cromwell and
of Richelieu did not lack great men or great artists, but the

mission of the latter was not exactly what it had been. What they accomplished in the way of painting considered as an art for its own sake is best attested by the fact that the painters of that day are still the models and teachers of our own.

Among the names so far mentioned Velasquez stands among the foremost as the great student of men and of character, as shown by the medium of art. In his masterly subordination of details to essential facts and his large power of vision which carries the man to the canvas and fixes him there for all posterity, he can in general only find equals or rivals in Rembrandt and among the older Venetians or the very greatest names of the early Renaissance. Such art shows us again and again that

FIG. 164.—" The Divine Shepherd." Murillo. Madrid.

the pencil and brush are only means to an end, that technical facility in their use is admirable only when mind controls the hand.

It was the fortune or tact of Velasquez as a great realist, to steer clear of the religious subjects of his time. As we find these latter treated by Murillo we can only say that he rose to the highest level of his period and that this was not that of the sixteenth century. Our point of view for his "Divine Shepherd," for example, does not so much relate to the picture itself as to the fact that his period mainly never was more serious than it is here. Taking this picture as a picture, we find it charming; taking it as a conception of the Christ subject, we find it admissible or tolerable; taking it as an example of the tone of the period, we are reminded that this century did not succeed equally well in more intellectual or more serious conceptions.

The beauty of Murillo's pictures, their warmth, and tender devotional spirit will always find admirers. The most inexperienced eye takes pleasure in a Murillo. No higher praise could be paid this artist. We must also give high rank to the somber power of Ribera, or Spagnoletto, as he was also called. His "Jacob's Ladder" is an excellent illustration of the semi-romantic spirit of the time and of the class and style of scripture subject in which this spirit was most successful. We could not wish that this picture had another name, and yet it is doubtful if it does not more successfully transfer us to the world of dreams at large than to the world and days of Genesis.

Beside these Spaniards, the Flemings, Rubens and Van Dyck, take in their own way an equal rank. In portraits, landscapes, mythologic and religious subjects, Rubens was a prolific and vigorous producer. Italian influences had been long ascendant on the art of Flanders, but Rubens was the first who knew how to graft the color and science of the foreign art on a Flemish stock without sacrificing his own native spontaneity and Flemish character. The "Descent from the Cross," in the Antwerp Cathedral, was his greatest picture.

His pupil, Van Dyck, shows still more distinctly the reflex of his Italian models. Like Rubens, the friend of courts and kings, his peculiar forte was to portray the aristocratic and royal people of his day. In religious art he had not the strength or earnestness of Rubens and only in special cases, as in our illustration from Antwerp, did he rise to the level of his master's religious pictures. As a colorist, how-

FIG. 105.—Detail from a Holy Family. By Rubens. Pitti Palace.

ever, he may be considered the superior of Rubens in refinement and in harmony.

In the Italian painting of this age the painters of Naples and Bologna took the lead, displacing the civic centers of earlier times. The former carried to the highest pitch a bold realism which has caused them to be named the School of the Naturalists, while the Bolognese are also known as the "Eclectics," that is, universalists or imitators. As this designation would imply, their art was academic and "correct," but lacking in spontaneity and in originality.

In the typical religious subjects of these Italians we find the tide of taste turning toward those which favor the ecstatic or the sentimental. The isolated Magdalens, the Immaculate Conceptions, Ecce Homos (heads of the Savior crowned with thorns), half-figures or heads of saints and Madonnas are of this period. The same holds of the isolated crucifixion scenes.

According to the ordinary presumptions of people who have not studied the topic, such pictures were typical for all old religious art, but the contrary is the case. In the early sixteenth century the actual crucifixion was rarely rendered. The "Deposition from the Cross" replaced it. At that time the Head of Christ is unknown, likewise the Head of the Madonna. The "Immaculate Conception" type is also unknown to the great period of Italian art, so

FIG. 106.—Madonna, by Guido Reni. Uffizi Gallery, Florence.

are the Magdalens as a half-figure type. One by Titian is a solitary exception. His "Assumption of the Madonna" is the only important case of its time.

In sixteenth century instances where the ecstatic expression is attempted, as in Raphael's "Transfiguration" (Fig. 84), and Titian's "Assumption" (Fig. 95), the great dignity and reserve are to be noted and compared with seventeenth century types. In the same sense the reserve and dignity of the "Sistine Madonna" by Raphael may be compared with the Immaculate Conceptions. All these facts point to the larger, more general one, that good taste and common sense have not been confined to the nineteenth century, and that as far as religious painting is concerned they have never been so prominent since as they were in

FIG. 107.—The Annunciation. Sassoferrato. Louvre.

the sixteenth century Italian art. Good taste avoids the painfully tragic; common sense avoids the ecstatic and the sentimental, or handles it with great reserve.

The landscapes, mythologic scenes, and "genre" pictures (realistic subjects) are the most successful of this time. In these the period announced its own tastes and preferences most clearly, while the traditional religious pictures were largely a cloak and disguise for a realistic art lacking real sympathy with the heart of the subject and consequently treating it without earnestness.

In landscapes and classical subjects the Frenchmen, Claude Lorrain and Nicholas Poussin, respectively took first rank, both residents and students in Italy.

Among the Bolognese, headed by the three artists of the Caracci family, we specify as specially important names those of Guido Reni, Domenichino, and Guercino. Among the "Naturalists" we mention Salvator Rosa and Caravaggio (to whom the Spaniard Ribera, long resident in Naples, is also generally reckoned). The leading picture of its century is Guido's fresco of the "Dawn" or "Aurora," on the ceiling of the Rospigliosi Villa at Rome. The greatest work of Domenichino is the "Diana and Nymphs" of the Borghese Gallery.

Guido Reni on the whole deserves first place among the Italians of this age. He was an industrious and able manufacturer of all the classes of pictures which I have specified as types. His Magdalens, Ecce Homos, Crucifixions, and Immaculate Conceptions

FIG. 108.—Saint Cecilia. By Sassoferrato. Venice Academy.

are very numerous. In the Crucifixion type he had an active follower in Van Dyck. In the Immaculate Conceptions Murillo carried off the palm.

The names of the Italians Sassoferrato and Carlo

Dolci represent a weaker art, which unhappily offers excellent subjects for photographs and engravings, tending by their clearness and distinctness in copy to give an unduly important place to the originals.

In treating of the seventeenth century we must always keep two points in view; first, to be just to its own great excellence and achievements; second, not to be unjust to its great predecessor, and to preserve a proper perspective in our notions of the two.

FIG. 109.—Detail from Diana's Chase. Domenichino. Borghese Gallery. Rome.

The difficulty in preserving this perspective lies partly in the fact that the galleries of northern Europe necessarily exhibit a larger number of the later pictures, which are seen by many to whom the monumental works of Italy are not so familiar. The copies and reproductions of these seventeenth century works are also more in demand because they are better known, and because being smaller in original they make relatively larger and more decorative copies.

It is the universal experience of students that as beginners they are first drawn to the art of the seventeenth century. In external and momentary attractiveness it undoubtedly holds its own. This should scarcely be reckoned against it; but "still waters run deep" and the waters of the seventeenth century are rarely still, at least in the religious art of Italy. For genuine and spontaneous feeling in this century we shall fare best with the French, the Spaniards, the Flemings, and the Dutch. The English had as yet no painters of their own worth naming. (Sir Peter Lely and Godfrey Kneller were Germans.)

FIG. 110.—Portrait of Lucas Baumgärtner. Albert Dürer. Munich.

CHAPTER XXI.

OUR most natural first attitude toward early northern art is to use it as a foil for the contemporary Italian. We can appreciate Masaccio and Da Vinci at their best when we compare them with Van der Weyden or Albert Dürer. But this attitude is followed by another, the recognition of old German sincerity, honesty, and truth as attested by old German pictures. There is also an imaginative quality in German art which the Italian lacked, often disguised in fantastic and grotesque forms, but still thoughtful and profound.

The German art of the early sixteenth century was also Renaissance. It also shared, and succeeded in, the effort to return to nature and to revive the science of design. It also felt the influence of classic thought and literature and experienced the influence of Italy. Albert Dürer studied in Venice and the Renaissance traits are very clear in Holbein. But German art was more tardy than Italian, and in the early sixteenth century it is still so distinctly and peculiarly national that we can only remotely relate it to the larger movement.

These main things have to be said of German painting: First, that in face of the stained-glass windows of the northern Gothic its beginnings were much crippled by their rivalry. That wall surface of the churches which the Italian gave up to painting, the northerner gave up to stained glass. Hence for the fifteenth century, German and Netherland art was confined to panels for altar pictures, mostly of extremely small size. In general the medieval and Gothic ignorance of form was still the rule in the fifteenth century, though here we must distinguish in favor of the Netherlands as against Germany.

In the early sixteenth century when the two great names of Albert Dürer and Hans Holbein are in question for South Germany, we must give them place more as phenomenal geniuses for their given time and surroundings, less as highest representatives of an otherwise average excellence. Yet it is possible that a German critic would not draw this line.

Fig. 111.—Woodcut by Albert Dürer.

In Dürer there was, aside from his not always successful struggle to throw off the bondage of German medieval tradition, a peculiar fantastic method and spirit individual to himself, and this we need to understand and discount. He was at his best in woodcuts and mainly active in this branch of art. His comparatively rare oil paintings are distinguished by marvelous painstaking minuteness, strong sense of character, and highly trained facility in use of the brush and pencil.

Hans Holbein belonged to a later generation, one more familiar as a whole with the new science and art of Italy, but he does not in any sense deny his birth-right. Obvious Italian influence is confined to the architectural details of his paintings (for instance the niche of the famous Meier Madonna in Dresden). He was much more successful than Dürer in obtaining commissions for oil paintings, many of which are in Basle, others in Hampton Court and other English collections, still others in various galleries. The most famous of all is the

Fig. 112.—The Flagellation. Woodcut by Albert Dürer.

large Madonna in Dresden, although this painting is now thought to be a copy of its counterpart in Darmstadt.

Holbein was also an active designer of woodcuts, which just then were very popular in the North both for Bible subjects and other illustrative purposes. He also figured as a successful fresco painter both in London and in Basle, but all his wall-paintings have gone to ruin or have been destroyed.

A very slight acquaintance with these German painters will show their value for history. The quality and character of the people come to us through their art with marvelous suggestiveness.

We cannot quote for the Netherland sixteenth century, names of equal distinction with the great South Germans. Quentin Matsys is here the leading name—an artist sharing with many of his countrymen the strange and suggestive trait of showing two entirely distinct styles, an earlier style of the old Flemish and Germanic quality and a later one borrowed wholesale from Italian models. The Italian influence was not, however, successfully assimilated in

FIG. 113.—Portrait of Hans Holbein by himself. Uffizi Gallery. Florence.

the sixteenth century, and we have seen that the distinction of Rubens lay in this assimilation.

CHAPTER XXII.

SEVENTEENTH CENTURY DUTCH PAINTING.

PASSING by the seventeenth century Flemings already mentioned, we now turn to the Dutch painters of the same era.

In Holland, art at any earlier date is mainly conspicuous by its absence or when rarely found is a repetition of that common to early Flanders and Germany; but in the seventeenth century this country produced the most remarkable school of painting then known in Europe.

Not only does Holland boast in the person of Rembrandt, an artist who was at least equal to the greatest of his time, but a host of other lights, among whom Franz Hals, Ruisdael, Jan Steen, Brouwer, Adrian van

FIG. 114.—Franz van Mieris. Portrait of the Artist and his Wife. The Hague.

Ostade, Netscher, Metsu, Peter Hoogh, Franz and Willem van Mieris, Paul Potter, Cuyp, Van Goyen, Terburg are a few only out of many whose names may not be always

so familiar, but whose works in the Gallery of Amsterdam
show them the equals or rivals of these.

The phenomenal development of Dutch art has a historic
explanation which has best been given by an American

FIG. 115.—Cattle. Paul Potter. The Hague.

author.* The sum of this explanation is that Holland
led the world in science, industry, and commerce for the
given time and that her art is one reflex of this larger fact.

The character of this art is peculiarly original, in fact
absolutely phenomenal, when precedent and tradition are
considered. In the early days of the Protestants there was
a general prejudice against church paintings and religious
art decoration which we no longer share but which was

* Already quoted. Douglas Campbell, " The Puritan in Holland, England, and
America." See also Taine, " Art in the Netherlands."

long ascendant.   Hence Protestantism led to the abjuring
of religious art but elsewhere had found no substitute for it.
Painting practically disappeared from Germany as a consequence of this religious prejudice after the death of
Holbein and Lucas Cranach.   In England it had no flower
till the eighteenth century.

In Holland only did the Protestant artist seek in the
life about him the subject matter which tradition could
no longer supply.   The life of the house and farm, of

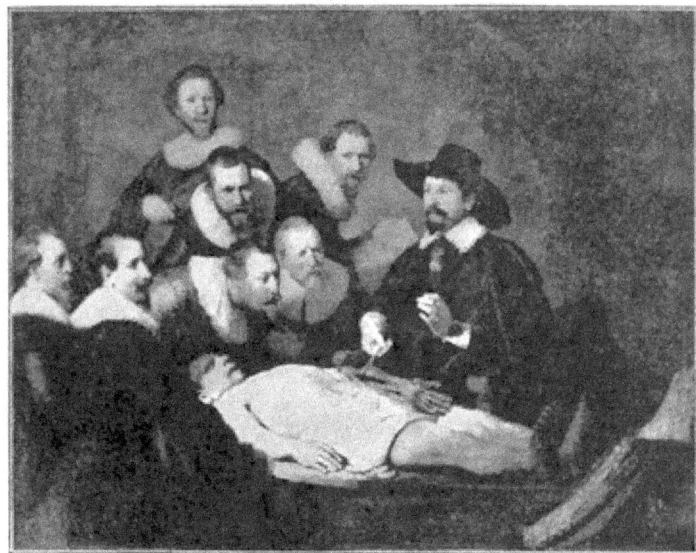

Fig. 116.—The Anatomy Lesson. Rembrandt. The Hague.

kitchen and parlor, of the village, the city, and the town,
of the sailor and the soldier, of the doctor, the tradesman,
and the tavern, of the animal and the flower, of the corporation, the guild, and the patrol—this was what the Dutch

artist carried to his canvas.   In his pictures, conscience, honesty, and truth to nature are the ever conspicuous traits.

Among Dutch paintings the "Corporation pictures" claim our first notice.   These give the associated portraits

FIG. 117.—Banquet of the Officers of the Archers' Corps of St. Adrian.
Franz Hals.   Haarlem.

of the leaders of the various guilds, officers of the military companies, heads of the hospitals, charitable asylums and the like, and often the portrait figures are full length and united in some activity peculiar to the association.

Rembrandt's "Anatomy Lesson" at The Hague belongs to a class of pictures representing the associations of the doctors, to which this motive of an anatomical lecture and demonstration was common.   One entire room in the Amsterdam Gallery is filled with similar pictures, all illustrating the transcendent genius of Rembrandt, who has caused them to be forgotten.

To a like class of paintings belong Rembrandt's "Cloth Merchants" at Amsterdam, and the famous series by Franz Hals at Haarlem.   Rembrandt's "Night Watch" at Amsterdam is one of hundreds of similar pictures of the patrols and military bands.   It represents Captain Franz Banning Cocq's company of arquebusiers emerging from their guild house.

These instances have value as show-ing a parallel to the conditions of Italian art, and a similar re-lation of popularity and public interest.

In a domestic art for the home and the pri-vate dwelling Holland was also an innovator. Earlier paintings had existed for public build-ings, churches, and palaces.   Domestic art in the modern sense had been previously unknown.   In Ger-many woodcuts had taken its place.   In

Fig. 118.—Portrait. Rembrandt. Amsterdam.

Italy the need of it had not been felt while churches and public buildings were open to the people.

The trivial, anecdotal, and commonplace subjects of the Dutch painters thus become an interesting turning point in

FIG. 119.—The Doctor's Visit. Jan Steen. The Hague.

the history of civilization. It is rarely, however, that we do not find a point to the story or a permanent interest attaching to the scenes from daily life. In fact these pictures are better than an open book for the study of old Dutch civilization. A large proportion of these paintings are of small dimensions as befitting their trivial and domestic subjects. In these small pictures the methods of execution are refined and painstaking to the point of

FIG. 120.—Dutch Landscape. Ruisdael. Amsterdam.

nicety. In larger pictures, as for instance those of Hals and Rembrandt, the method changes and becomes broad and masterly. In color and design the old Dutch artists can still give points to most modern painters. Their greatest works are still unrivaled.

Here again as in the earlier case of Italian art, we do not concede that native genius is lacking to our own time. We

FIG. 121.—Tavern Scene. David Teniers the Younger. The Hague.

only point to the fact that public national interest and support create an art and essentially determine its character. No one could deny that for the given area and number of people, the production of pictures in seventeenth century Holland was more active, their number greater, their relation to the actual lives of everyday people closer and more genuine, than in any country of our own time. Whoever has conceded this has also conceded that an average superiority of old Dutch art to our own was a natural consequence.

On the other hand the range of Dutch subjects belonged to that class which is most popular to-day, the domestic and the anecdotal, the landscape and the scene from real life.

It is interesting to see that as early as the seventeenth century the essential features of the nineteenth century painting were thus anticipated and prefigured.

Many pictures analogous in subjects to those affected by the Dutch were painted by the Flemings of the same period. It is in the matter of religious art that the two schools especially fell asunder. David Teniers the Younger, whose tavern scenes are world-famous, is the most obvious illustration of the close relations often existing between Dutch and Flemish art.

CHAPTER XXIII.

RENAISSANCE SCULPTURE.

Relations to Modern History.

It may be regretted that a division of topics according to different arts seems to detract from that general view of one given century as a whole and of a series of sequent centuries, each massed in contrast with the others, which it should be our main effort to create. On the other hand, there is a certain cumulative result in such a treatment, which with each new art demonstrates the repetition of the same essential facts for a given time.

Each art, whether sculpture, painting, or architecture, exhibited in fifteenth century Italy the same simplicity, the same reserve, the same faithful striving after proportion and scientific accuracy. Each art in the early sixteenth century showed the same transcendent mastery of means as applied to ends, the same culmination of power and mass, the same triumphant self-assertion of a new-born modern civilization. Each art in the seventeenth century exhibited a similar striving for effect, a similar exaggeration of the picturesque quality, a similar disposition to exalt the means above the end and the parts above the whole.

If our parallel breaks for this century when extended to Dutch painting, it holds throughout the whole of Europe otherwise, and will even hold for Dutch painting if we stretch the limit into the eighteenth century when this art lost every element of its earlier vitality and power. In the eighteenth century England took the place in art, but not in the same high degree, which had in the sixteenth century belonged to Italy, and which had in the seventeenth century belonged to Holland, Spain, and Flanders.

In all these arts we take the same general point of view regarding these gradual changes, that art as a whole filled a larger place in daily use and thought before printing substituted a new means of expression, before modern national states obliterated the rivalries and ambitions of civic communities, before the enlargement of the general field of science tended to specialize the individual, to dwarf the symmetry of character and the wide personal experience which are the best education for the artist in design.

In the large dimensions of our great modern countries it may be possible for a musical composer or a great author to keep in touch with an entire nation. Bret Harte, Dickens, or Whittier, or the composers of those street ballads of our day which we affect to despise and which will go down to history as some of our greatest and purest efforts of art; Beethoven, Mozart, and Mendelssohn—such men may still claim a hold over an entire nation or even an entire civilization, for the power of music is not fettered by the bond of language. But our numbers are too large and our distances too great for a painting, statue, or building to master the admiration of a whole nation. The book or the musical composition is susceptible of multiplication and diffusion; not so the work of art which is seen. At first hand, it can only be known in one example.

It may be added that our culture is too complex and the eyes of most of us too dull. The artist is, and always will be, the spokesman of his audience. His inspiration and success will correspond to the enthusiasm and the interest of that audience. It is only a World's Fair which is also a Columbian celebration that can revive the conditions and

results which we know in the early Renaissance for the arts
of design as regards work done for the admiration, enjoy-
ment, and appreciation of an enormous multitude of people.

Once more, then, it is our duty to say that the history
of Renaissance art has a double meaning for our time.
First and foremost it means and represents modern civilization at large. In this sense it is representative for things
and facts which cannot be seen but which it may, neverthe-
less, imply—the science, industry, comforts, and manners
which have spread from Italy for all modern history.

In this sense Renaissance art has been perpetual. The
science of our builder will go back to it, however the
external form may change, and even this external form,
as we have seen, has been perpetuated in architecture.
A Rembrandt, a Reynolds, or a Rousseau may abjure
every outward trait of Italian art and still owe every stroke
of his brush to its inspiration. So likewise the modern
sculptor cannot sever his connection with the time which
revived the study of anatomy and the science of form.

On the other hand, when the arts of design are considered
in and for themselves we must still in each art confess the
general superiority of the early Renaissance to ourselves.

In certain cases it must be admitted that our modern
American sculptors push it hard. With adequate patronage it is difficult to say how far they might not go in rivalry
or in superiority; whereas in painting it is difficult to
see how later time can equal the Renaissance, unless the
same subject matter could be revived; for an art must
ultimately be judged by its subject matter, and no subject
matter can be imagined equal to that which the Bible subjects once offered for painting. All, however, that can be
asked of any art or of any century is that it be true to itself
and to its opportunities.

CHAPTER XXIV.

Critical Review.

As WE are dealing in comparisons and with a view to understanding both ourselves and the past, let it be said here what is the greatest virtue of the early Italian sculpture.

The first notion of the novice in criticism is that art is judged by a certain amount of technical perfection and of positive science. It is difficult or impossible to imagine from this point of view why one artist possessing the requisite positive science might not always equal another possessing the same amount of science, and difficult to see why the same talent and the

FIG. 122.—Swathed Infant in Enameled Terra Cotta. By Andrea della Robbia. From the Architectural Decorations of the Loggia dei Innocenti. Florence. Fifteenth Cent.

same effort might not always reach the same point of science.

To the first difficulty we answer, that technical science in

199

art up to a point of comparative perfection is assumed to start with, by the historic critic. The modern is supposed to possess it before he could reach the distinction of making a publicly exhibited work. That is the affair of the schools and the exhibitions. The old artist must have possessed it to have won a place in the estimation of centuries. The historic critic does not worry himself over the slips in drawing which a modern can point out in the "Last Judgment." He is satisfied with knowing that no modern has drawn, could draw, or can draw, a similar number of variously fore-shortened figures without making more mistakes. We do not take the trouble to correct the grammar of Shakespeare.

Fig. 123.—Equestrian Statue of Gattamelata. By Donatello. Padua. Fifteenth Century.

What is then in question in our admiration for Ghiberti or Luca della Robbia if it be not the technical science?

The answer is that all classic art, whether in music, literature, or design, is conditioned by a sentiment of personal unconsciousness or simplicity and of absorption in the subject matter. All these arts exist to awaken or create ideas. The form exists for the sake of a meaning. If then the "Annunciation" of a Robbia relief, the "Christ and Peter Walking on the Water," on the first Ghiberti doors, or the equestrian portrait of "Gattamelata" by Donatello has that stamp of unconsciousness and of simplicity, or of great power, which art carries with it when the meaning fills and transcends the form, we pronounce these works classic because the artist has made his technical science the means to an end and has achieved it by sinking his own personality in his subject (Figs. 123, 125, 129).

Great art is generally simple, the greatest art invariably so. It is the unconsciousness and ease of good breeding that we demand from a work of art—and just as good breeding

FIG. 124.—Christ Healing the Sick. Architectural Medallion in Enameled Terra Cotta. By Andrea and Luca della Robbia. Florence. Fifteenth Century.

is the non-obtrusion and the unconsciousness of self so it is in art. Its standard is the conquest of self in behalf of the subject matter. Then comes the question, "What is that subject matter?" and according to its value so ranks the work of art.

Our standards are the same and our point of view the same in the matter of early Italian painting, but it is much more difficult to illustrate a painting, whereas we can fairly reproduce the sculpture in a photograph, especially if the

composition be simple.   As far as pictures are concerned
as related to the actual text of my book, I cannot anywhere
make my meaning so clear or force the reader to admira-
• tion and respect simply by illustration, as I can with the
statuary art of the Italian fifteenth century.   Its charm of
unconsciousness is too palpable to be ignored, too evident
to be overlooked, and too beautiful to escape appreciation.
Let us choose our examples first where the point is
clearest ; the "Madonna with Angels," by Luca della
Robbia (Fig. 126), the "Annunciation," by Andrea della

FIG. 125.—The Annunciation.   Relief in Enameled Terra Cotta.   By Andrea
della Robbia.   Prato.   Fifteenth Century.

Robbia (Fig. 125), "Christ Healing the Sick," by Luca
and Andrea della Robbia (Fig. 124), the "Swathed In-

fant," by Andrea della Robbia (Fig. 122), the "Madonna,"
probably by Mino da Fiesole (Fig. 139).

Now this trait of unconsciousness and simplicity does not
lie solely in the genius of the individual artist, it lies also in •

FIG. 126,—Lunette in Enameled Terra Cotta. By Luca della Robbia.   Still in
position over a Florentine Doorway.   Madonna and Child
with Angels.   Fifteenth Century.

the genius of a period.   The whole Greek sculpture is
saturated with it until we reach the decadence of Greek
sculpture, and by the absence of that quality that decadence
is fixed and determined.   This trait is the essential deter-
minant in our estimate of Dutch painting.   Its absence
fixes the place of the Italian art of the seventeenth century.
Compare the "Annunciation" by Sassoferrato (Fig. 107),
with the "Annunciation" by Andrea della Robbia.   Compare the Madonnas of Guido, or of Carlo Dolci with those
of the Robbias and of Mino da Fiesole.

We will return now to the presumed case of the novice, who supposes that scientific and technical perfection fixes the place of a work of art, and declare that this perfection ✱ has little to do with it. For wherever the mission exists which needs to find an utterance in art, there will the tools be found to make this utterance, and the conscience which will learn the use of those tools up to the point required.

It is difficult to believe that hundreds on hundreds of paintings, all in fact painted in the greatest time of Italian art, bear this quality to view of unconsciousness, of ingenuous sincerity, of absorption in the subject matter for its own sake, but so it is. It long outlasted the time of Michael Angelo's "Last Judgment" in Venetian paintings and otherwise mainly disappeared from Italian art after 1530. In fifteenth century Italian sculpture it is the conspicuous and obvious charm.

CHAPTER XXV.

EARLY RENAISSANCE SCULPTURE.

Historic Sketch.

THE earliest dawn of modern feeling for nature and of interest in ancient sculpture as an assistance to its study is found with Nicolo of Pisa and in his pulpit made for the Baptistery in Pisa about the year 1260. His son Giovanni carried this feeling and this interest into the fourteenth century and headed a school of artists whose works are found in many parts of Italy.* Among these one of the most important is the pair of bronze doors made for the Florence Baptistery by Andrea Pisano with panel compositions from the life of John the Baptist. The designs of Giotto for reliefs on the Florence Cam-

Fig. 127.—The Baptistery of Florence. The Doors on the left by Andrea Pisano; those on the right are the second pair by Ghiberti.

panile (bell-tower of the Cathedral), are also works of great

---

* " Roman and Medieval Art," Figs. 126, 127, 128, 131.

power and interest.* In the main, however, fresco painting had absorbed the activity of fourteenth century Italian
art. The best comparison for the average Italian sculpture
in relief during the fourteenth century with that now to
be considered, is offered by an illustration quoted in foot-
note for the works of Giovanni Pisano and scholars at
Orvieto. For statues the "Madonna" by Giovanni Pisano
at Prato, quoted in foot-note, offers a similar typical contrast which will hold good for other works.

In our detailed account of fifteenth century Italian sculpture we begin with the
opening of the century
and the first pair of
bronze doors made by
Lorenzo Ghiberti for
the Baptistery in Flor-
ence (1403–1424).

The pictorial beauty
and more realistic de-
tails of the second pair
of doors by the same
artist, have tended to
obscure the importance
of these earlier ones.
They are often over-
looked by travelers
and by illustrators.
No cast of them can be

FIG. 128.—Christ and the Money Changers.
Bronze Relief Panel. From the first
pair of Doors by Ghiberti.

seen in this country; but the power of the compositions is
at least equal, if not superior, to those subsequently made.
The compositions are simpler, more circumscribed and

* "Roman and Medieval Art," Figs. 129, 130—the execution of the latter is by
Luca della Robbia.

more concentrated. For the designs of "Christ and the Money Changers" and "Christ and Peter Walking on the Water," our illustrations will speak, and speak eloquently.

It would be difficult to mention more powerful compositions in the whole range of Christian art (Figs. 128, 129).

The commission for the second and more famous pair of bronze doors was undertaken in 1425 and completed in 1452, so that fifty years' labor was altogether devoted to these two works of art.

Should the question arise as to a comparison between our mod-

FIG. 129.—"Christ and Peter Walking on the Water." Bronze Relief Panel from the first pair of Ghiberti's Doors.

ern artists and Ghiberti, it would be unfair to judge the former until some modern city or national government is willing to allot an equal amount of time and proportionate payment for the creation of similar works of art. The willingness to wait twenty-seven years for the completion of one commission and to pay large yearly stipends for that length of time both to Ghiberti and to his numerous assistants tells the whole story of the perfection of early Renaissance art.

The general appearance of the panels and surrounding borders of the second pair of bronze doors is best explained by the illustrations. In these panels are repre-

sented important events of Old Testament history—the
Creation, story of Cain and Abel, story of Noah, story
of Abraham, etc.   For the great beauty of the compositions in these panels, for instance in the story of Jacob
and Esau or the story of Joseph, we can scarcely find
parallels outside the much later works of Raphael.   For
the pose and designs of single figures (story of Abraham,
story of Noah), we are not less at a loss for parallels
even when the sixteenth century is admitted to the comparison (Figs. 132, 133, 134, 135).

The marvel begins to fully reveal itself only when we
consider the dates and
look for parallels in the
art of Ghiberti's own
time.

The art of sculpture
logically precedes that
of painting, for the
form must be con-
ceived as a solid before
it can be transferred in
outline to a flat surface.
No doubt the whole
fifteenth century sculp-
ture is superior to the
contemporary paint-

FIG. 130.—Design for a Bronze Door Panel by
Brunellesco. The Sacrifice of Isaac. Florence.

ing, but again the mar-
vel is that Ghiberti
should, as the first among moderns, have reached a point
of perfection in his figure compositions which the nineteenth
century has not rivaled.

We have seen that the frescoes of Masaccio in the Brancacci Chapel date between 1423 and 1428, but in the com-

positions for the first Ghiberti doors we go back to 1403. The more we know of preceding fourteenth century art, the more the wonder grows in spite of various connecting links which here and there can be established.

We know, however, of a competition of designs as having been held for the selection of the artist of the first bronze doors in question, and that three artists besides Ghiberti entered this contest. The competitive design of Brunellesco, whom we shall remember as the first great architect of the Renaissance (p. 72), is still preserved in Florence beside the prize design of Ghiberti; both subjects from the Sacrifice of Isaac. The story goes that the judges were unable

Fig. 131.—Design for a Bronze Door Panel by Ghiberti. The Sacrifice of Isaac. Florence.

to decide until Brunellesco himself gave judgment against himself and retired from the competition (Figs. 130, 131).

Later criticism has universally conceded the superior dignity and beauty of the panel by Ghiberti. Still we see that he was by no means absolutely isolated in the perfection of his art at the beginning of the fifteenth century.

Remembering Brunellesco as the first great reviver of ancient forms in architecture, it is interesting to notice in Ghiberti's designs (story of Joseph, story of Jacob and Esau) the classic details of the buildings and to relate the

FIG. 132.—Second pair of Bronze Doors by Ghiberti.   Florence Baptistery.

spirit which copied them to that which had such perception for nature and for beauty and such science in re-creating them. The double character of the Renaissance, enthusiasm for antiquity and enthusiasm for visible nature, thus appears in this one work. The influence of ancient art is also seen in the pose and draping of the figures. Those

FIG. 133.—The Story of Jacob and Esau. Detail from the second pair of Bronze Doors by Ghiberti.

especially of the allegorical figures of the borders, as being of somewhat larger size than the figures of the panel compositions, offer clear illustration of this point (Figs. 133, 134, 135).

Among the medallion heads of these borders are portraits of leading Florentine artists, Ghiberti's own among them.

The outer framework of the door is a wonderful illustration of realistic science, while the details as placed in combination show an antique influence in arrangement. Casts of these details are still frequently used in schools of art as models for the modern student (Fig. 136).

It is habitual for critical writers to allude to the departure from relief style which Ghiberti allowed himself in these bronze doors. They undoubtedly show an amount of pictorial detail which goes beyond the theoretic limits

FIG. 134.—Sacrifice of Isaac. Abraham and the Angels. Hagar and Ishmael in the Desert. Detail from the second pair of Bronze Doors by Ghiberti.

proper for a solid material like bronze and for sculptured relief as practiced by the Greeks. It is hardly worth while, however, even to mention such a point. The significance of the work is pictorial. It illustrates the realism of the

Renaissance and the precedence of Ghiberti in that realism. Its main influence was undoubtedly pictorial, and we should consider it the great landmark of the Renaissance art of

FIG. 135.—The Story of Joseph and his Brethren. Detail from the second pair of Bronze Doors by Ghiberti.

design in general rather than confine our point of view to sculpture and the canons of Greek relief.

There is still something to be said of the Ghiberti doors. We notice in their panels a combination of episodes in one field. This is seen in the story of Joseph, the story of Jacob and Esau, the story of Abraham, the story of Noah. This combination occurs without indications of local division, although the localities are conceived in all these cases, except the story of Joseph and story of Jacob, as various and distinct. In these last cases the episodes are also distinct in time, though not in place.

We have here a method which also constantly occurs in Italian fresco and which is an inheritance from the earliest Christian art—an illustration of its ideal standpoint and of its independence of illusion even when realism had become a controlling interest. Such arrangement was obviously conducive to balanced composition in large panels, whether of frescoed walls or otherwise. It admitted brief and simple characterization of each special story and gave the work of art a comprehensive effect.

We find this method continuing in the sixteenth century art. Raphael's "Transfiguration" includes the double story of the possessed boy and of the Transfiguration itself, events locally separate but spiritually related, since the disciples could not cast out the devil in the absence of the Savior. Michael Angelo represented the "Temptation and Expulsion from Eden" on one panel of the Sistine Chapel ceiling. Countless parallel cases could be instanced. For example, in the Sistine Madonna, by Raphael, we have actually represented the dream or vision of the pope who is kneeling in the picture.

Fig. 136.—Decorative Details from the outer Framework of the second pair of Bronze Doors by Ghiberti.

Before leaving the bronze doors of Ghiberti we must

FIG. 137.—Equestrian Statue of Colleoni. By Verocchio. Venice. Fifteenth Century.

allude to the curious fate which has given not only precedence in time, but an actually unique importance in the matter of parallel works to this single one. It did not happen that any similar commission was undertaken in any other Italian city within the limits of the great period. Other bronze doors, for instance of the Pisa Cathedral, belong to a time when overcrowded compositions and excess of small details had quite overpowered the sentiment for simplicity of effect. The doors of Ghiberti not only stand first, but they stand alone in their perfection for the given class of works.

We must place as next in time and importance to these works the colossal equestrian portrait statues executed by Donatello and Verocchio, both Floren-

FIG. 138.—Bust of Nicolo da Uzzano. By Donatello. Fifteenth Century.

tines, and later contemporaries of Ghiberti and Brunellesco.
Donatello's statue of the Venetian mercenary captain, Gattamelata, is in Padua (1453). Verocchio's statue of the
Venetian captain, Colleoni, is in Venice (1476). These
two equestrian figures are not only the first but also
undoubtedly the greatest of modern history and are so
generally considered; that of Verocchio is the inimitable
masterpiece of all equestrian statues. For Donatello's own
masculine and sturdy character as well as for the noble
quality of his art, the bust illustrated by Fig. 138 will also
serve as an example.

Donatello ranks in
time and general sig-
nificance as the most
important sculptor pre-
ceding Michael An-
gelo, but the position
claimed by the Floren-
tine, Luca della Robbia
and his nephew, An-
drea, would seem to
make them more fairly
the subjects for repre-
sentative illustration of
Italian art at large
during the same period.

Luca della Robbia
was a successful artist
both in bronze and
marble. In the latter

FIG. 139.—Marble Shrine Relief of the Madonna
and Child in Vienna. Florentine Work. Fifteenth Century. School of Mino da Fiesole.

material are his well-known reliefs for the balustrade of
the organ-loft of the Florence Cathedral which are now in
Florence as museum exhibits. But it was in the glazed or

enameled terra cotta reliefs in color, which he was the first to execute, that he won especial renown.

This art was practiced by several and successive members of his family and flourished till about 1525. It then died out and has never been rediscovered or revived. The peculiarly unpretentious and simple style of these works is beyond all praise. They were used for decoration of exterior brick architecture, as medallions between arches, as lunettes in the arched spaces over doorways, etc., and also for altar-pieces, tombs, and votive tablets. Considering the inadequate effect of photographs from paintings, there is no access to a knowledge of early Italian art like that conveyed by photographs of these reliefs (Figs. 122, 124, 125, 126).

In marble reliefs, mainly of Madonnas, a peculiarly lovely phase of early Florentine art is also illustrated. Mino da Fiesole, Desiderio da Settignano, and Benedetto da Majano were the representative artists for this class of work.

CHAPTER XXVI.

RENAISSANCE SCULPTURE.

Philosophy of its Decline.

WE have still a thought to offer regarding the sculpture of the early Renaissance, one which suggests itself through the illustrations of Donatello's "St. George" and of the

FIG. 140.—St. George. By Donatello. Florence. Fifteenth Century.

"Davids" by Donatello and Verocchio (Figs. 141, 142), all of which are works held in high estimation by students of this period. This thought concerns the distinction between the statues of this period as works of art considered for themselves, as illustrations of its science of design and great advance over ages preceding, and the same statues considered in their historic relation to the whole art of the period and in their relation to the later position of sculpture among the arts of the Renaissance.

It is apparent that the subjects of Christian art do not

offer a large field for statues. As concerns close relation to Christian art it will be readily felt that the *reliefs* of the fifteenth century are most interesting and most distinctly related to their ostensible subject matter. In Donatello's "David" or "St. George" we have a class of subjects which soon exhausts itself and one where the appearance of the statue is but dimly related to our sympathies with the ostensible subject.

The number of such works is not large in the whole amount of the art of the Renaissance. Isolated statues of the Apostles or the Savior are not so interesting as a painting of the "Last Supper" or the cartoons of Raphael from the lives of the Apostles. The

Fig. 141.—David, by Verocchio. Florence. Fifteenth Century.

pictorial reliefs of Ghiberti from the story of Joseph are more interesting in their relation to subject matter than statues of David. Christian art has always found its most sympathetic field in painting or pictorial sculpture, that is in relief.

Sculpture offers the readiest illustration of Renaissance science. It preceded painting in the matter of high perfection. (On the other hand let us not forget that many of the great sculptors of the fifteenth century were also painters. This holds of Verocchio and Pollajuolo (Fig. 69), for instance.) The sculptors' studies were the basis of all the progress that painting made at this time and of the perfection which it reached a generation later, because they conditioned the scientific study of form ; but in the later Renaissance we detect a greater and greater ascendancy of the art of painting and the subjection of statuary to pictorial influence.

Statuary more and more became the work of isolated patronage and was ultimately rather the reflex of pictorial tendencies than an art for its own sake. This at least was its fate in the seventeenth and eighteenth centuries, when it sank to a condition of mediocrity and weakness far below the level of the contemporary pictures.

I should be inclined, therefore, to say that the paintings of the fifteenth century offer most matter for the historian ; the statues rather appeal to the special tastes of the art critic and the

FIG. 142.—David, by Donatello. Florence. Fifteenth Century.

student of design. They are certainly far less numerous, and it would be hard to find many parallels for the distinction of those which are illustrated, whereas in pictures

or in reliefs what one can offer in illustration is an infin-
itesimal suggestion of the actual production.

All this may serve as introduction to the topic of Michael
Angelo's sculpture and the sudden decline not only in
quality but also in productivity which followed his prodigious creations. The tomb monuments of the churches
supplied the main field of later activity for this art. In the
seventeenth century there was a revival in the amount of
production related to the general extravagance and luxury
of Catholic church decoration at this time, but the heart
and soul had then gone from the art. It was mostly
empty display and theatrical posturing.

CHAPTER XXVII.

Michael Angelo.

As A sculptor Michael Angelo stood on the shoulders of Donatello and Verocchio and added to their supreme science the passion, frenzy, and explosive power of his own volcanic nature. His peculiar quality is best appreciated from his later works, the Moses of San Pietro in Vinculi at Rome and the Tombs of the Medici in Florence.

The Moses is the most important figure and feature of the tomb of Pope Julius II., who was the artist's greatest patron and warmest appreciator. The whole character of Michael Angelo is revealed by his conception of Moses as witnessing the worship

FIG. 143.—Detail of the David by Michael Angelo, Florence.

of the golden calf; as about to spring from his seat and

222

dash to fragments the tablets of the law which had been revealed to him.

There is a closer relation to the history of his own time and his own life in this statue than we might suspect. In political life Michael Angelo had been a warm partisan

FIG. 144.—Moses, by Michael Angelo. Rome.

and the military commander for the Commonwealth of Florence in its final struggle and downfall (p. 36). He belonged then to the party of the old Republic and hated the party of foreign despotism and success. Commercial and money-making interests played no small part in this revolution. The Medici who were credited with having overthrown the liberties of Florence, belonged to the richest and most prominent banking family of that state. Spain and the Hapsburg dynasty of Austria were working in their interest.

What Michael Angelo saw as an Italian patriot was

FIG. 145.—Detail of the Tomb of Lorenzo Medici. By Michael Angelo.

the fast coming decadence of his country and a social revolution which had brought the meaner and more grasping tendencies of life to the front. His "Moses" was the protest against a worship of the golden calf which he saw in his own time and which had embittered his own life.

In the same way his Tombs of the Medici are well known to have been in his own view and that of his time, the tombs of the Florentine Republic. Made in the service and for the glory of a family which he hated, he disguised in these works the sorrow of the patriot and the regrets of the lost cause.

The tombs are those of the last two legitimate members of the Medici family, Giuliano and Lorenzo. Their seated figures are placed in niches, beneath which are the sarcophagi supporting respectively figures of "Dawn" and "Twilight," "Day and Night." "Dawn" and "Twilight" are allegories of the twilight of the expiring moments of life on earth and of the dawn of the spirit life. "Day" and "Night" are conceived as the antitheses of life and death. These tombs are in a chapel of the Florentine Church of San Lorenzo, whose erection by Brunellesco has been mentioned (p.73), and were finished about 1534.

FIG. 146.—Tomb of Lorenzo Medici. Florence. Allegorical Figures of Twilight and Dawn.

Of earlier date, about 1513, are the two "Captives" now in the Louvre. An entire series of these figures was to have surrounded the tomb of Julius II., emblematic of the arts and sciences held captive by Julius II. and dying with him. After the death of the pope the

diminished plan of his tomb made it impossible to connect
these finished figures with it, and they found their way
to France.

Here again the prophetic misanthropy of Michael Angelo
has its own inner meaning.   We have seen how the court
of Leo X. was one of
mainly borrowed
glories (p. 140), and
how the invasions of
Milan and Naples at
the close of the fifteenth
century had already in-
dicated the approach-
ing downfall of Italy.
The pontificate of Julius
II. was devoted to the
expulsion of the foreign
invaders of Italy. His
death was the signal
for new invasions whose
results after 1520 we
have described (pp.
35–41).   There is no
doubt that the political

FIG. 147.—Allegorical Figure of the Day, from
the Tomb of Giuliano Medici by
Michael Angelo.

foresight of the artist had its part in this allegory of the
Captives.   Certainly their prophecy was fulfilled.

Contortions and twistings of the human figure are the
sign manual of the artist's mood in most of these various
works, a reflex of his own irritability and unhappiness.
No doubt his anatomic studies and desire to produce
new and startling effects are also accountable for this
manner.   At all events he is the first artist in whom we
detect the disappearance of early Renaissance unconscious-

ness and simplicity. (See also notes on the "Last Judgment," p. 155.) The grandeur of his thought and conception makes it impossible to reckon this mannerism against him, but it infected the imitators and weaker followers of his greatness.

The inflated style of the decadence found its type in Michael Angelo. In his very protest against the coming epoch he was fated to influence its forms.

In the two greatest early works of this sculptor we find a more dignified and serener art. These are his colossal David in Florence and the Dead Savior in the lap of the Virgin* in St. Peter's at Rome. His earliest youthful work, the mask of a Faun, is still preserved in Florence. Here also are his statues of Bacchus and Adonis. The list of his important works also includes the Cupid at South Kensington in London, a Madonna in Bruges, and the Christ of the Church of Santa Maria Sopra Minerva in Rome.

The story of Michael Angelo's life as told by Vasari, who personally

Fig. 148.—Captive, by Michael Angelo.
Louvre.

knew him, is an almost essential thing to the compre-

---

* This typical subject is called by the Italians a " Pietà."

hension of his art. Deep piety and warm kindness of
heart were cloaked by surly manners and concealed by
solitude. I have already mentioned Grimm's ''Life of
Michael Angelo'' as giving not only the artist's life, but
also the political history of Italy as connected with it. It
also contains a summary of the whole Italian art history
of the time.

CHAPTER XXVIII.

RENAISSANCE SCULPTURE.

Later Styles and Decadence.

No SKETCH of Italian art could pass, without mention, the name of Benvenuto Cellini, the goldsmith and sculptor, whose greatest surviving work is the Perseus in Florence. Cellini was born in 1500, a quarter of a century after Michael Angelo. His statue dates from the middle of the sixteenth century, but the traditions and style of the great period still survive in this work. The art of sculpture in Italy at this time had otherwise generally sunk into relative affectation and mannerism.

FIG. 149.—Perseus, by Benvenuto Cellini. Florence.

In France we can quote serious and beautiful work from the hands of Goujon, Pilon, and others. A certain elongation of the figure and somewhat dainty elegance of conception which are visible in their works reflect the Italian style of the same day (Fig. 150).

We also notice the twisting of the figure as a trait constantly repeated in later art and borrowed originally from Michael Angelo. To an illustration of some of Goujon's

beautiful relief designs for a fountain in Paris, we must add
a renewed reference to some preceding pictures of French
Renaissance tomb sculpture and architectural statuary, all
of which will assist the reader to understand the Italian
quality, and origin of French and other modern sculpture
(Figs. 3, 10, 18).

It is difficult in a rapid summary to avoid oversights of
fine survivals of the
better and earlier
Italian Renaissance
style in later north
European Renaissance
art, but we must not
entirely forget the fine
Renaissance wood
carvings of Belgium
(Fig. 153). The tomb
of Queen Elizabeth in
Westminster Abbey
would also show how
far the Italian style had
traveled and how uni-
versal it had become.

In the early sixteenth
century Germany
boasted the important
names of Adam Krafft,

FIG. 150.—Figures from the Reliefs of the "Fountain of the Innocents." Paris. By Jean
Goujon. Middle of Sixteenth Century.

whose most famous works are the reliefs known as the
Seven Stations of the Cross, at Nuremberg, and Peter
Vischer, whose magnificent bronze tomb of St. Sebaldus is
in the church of the same name, also at Nuremberg. Out-
side of Nuremberg the most important works of German
Renaissance sculpture are at Innspruck, where the tomb

FIG. 151.—Mary of Burgundy (wife of Emperor Maximilian). From the series of Bronze Statues belonging to Maximilian's Monumental Tomb at Innspruck. By Gilg. Early Sixteenth Century.

of the Emperor Maximilian fills an entire church with the bronze figures of his ancestors and of the legendary heroes of medieval history.   Many German sculptors were employed on this colossal monument whose execution was in process during the whole sixteenth century.   One of the statues illustrated was probably a work by Peter Vischer.

For the later sculpture of Renaissance Europe down to the middle of the eighteenth century, I have selected five examples, not suggesting that anything but the broadest facts are indicated by them.   One of the latest of these, being the most obviously exaggerated and overstrained conception, may be first considered (Fig. 157).

FIG. 152.—King Arthur.   Bronze; by Peter Vischer.   From the Maximilian Monument at Innspruck.   Early Sixteenth Century.

It is a general rule of art criticism—first distinctly formulated and explained by the German critic Lessing, in his "Essay on Laocoön"—that a work of art should not exhaust its subject or so treat it that the extreme and ultimate pitch of emotion is made visible to the eye.

Moments of extreme tension are not lasting in their

nature, and when perpetuated in solid form they finally
become tedious; for the double reason that they present a
contradiction between the momentary duration in nature
and the permanence in art, and for the reason that in ex-

Fig. 153.—Wood-carved Confessionals at Antwerp. Church of St. Paul.
Late Sixteenth Century.

hausting the subject they leave nothing to the imagination.

In the *myth* of Prometheus, for instance, we are told the
story of a perpetual torture, but there is no existing Greek
statue of this subject, nor would any resembling our illustration have been possible for Greek views of art. The
given statue violates every rule of good taste, according to
our present training in criticism. It is vulgar, theatrical,
tawdry, and weak; but this is the style of sculpture which
ruled Europe down to the middle of the eighteenth century,
as an inheritance from the seventeenth century—and this

again had been led toward the downward road through the influence of the later sixteenth century.

From Michael Angelo on we become aware of an ever-increasing straining of attitudes, an ever-increasing choice of theatrical motives and sentimental subjects. The great master of this style was the seventeenth century Italian, Bernini, a man of great genius and great science, but a thorough man of his time; that is to say, absolutely destitute of the sentiment of the statuesque.

Let us also choose our next illustration from the eighteenth century, and consider its lessons (Fig. 156).

FIG. 154.—Æneas and Anchises, by Bernini. Borghese Villa, Rome. Seventeenth Century.

It is a fundamental rule of art that its tools are means to an end. Whatever exalts the instrument belittles the aim. Hence works of art which are made for the sake of conquering those difficulties which affect the use of tools have no real cause of being.

In our given illustration from a work in Naples, the subject was chosen because it gave the sculptor an opportunity of making a net in marble—an exceedingly difficult thing to do, but not worth doing. Probably this group offers the most remarkable example in statuary of the conquest of a technical

FIG. 155.—Pulpit of the Brussels Cathedral. Wood-carving by Verbruggen, about 1700. The Expulsion from Paradise.

difficulty, yet we feel that the entire subject has been
manufactured in order to create this difficulty.   As regards the ostensible subject matter, an allegory representing the "Escape from Error," it does not touch either
our interests, our sym-
pathies, or our con-
victions. Its only
possible claim to in-
terest is the dexterity
displayed in the use of
a chisel, and in artistic
value it is comparable
to the Chinese carvings
of ivory balls, con-
tained one within the
other.

This work, then,
may once more illus-
trate a general defect
of taste in statuary in
the seventeenth and
eighteenth centuries,
the tendency to exalt
the mechanics of art

FIG. 156.—The Escape from Error, by Queirolo.
Naples. Eighteenth Century.

while serious thought and conception were deficient.

In our illustration from the Cathedral of Brussels we have
an indication of the prodigality and luxury of sculpture
decoration in the important Catholic churches of the seventeenth century (Fig. 155).   It was a time when the multiplication of statues and carvings had no end; in many cases,
as here in the case of the pulpit, extorting our admiration
in spite of our better judgment; or, as also here, with re-
deeming traits when we consider the material used—for we

Fig. 157.—Prometheus, by Adam. Louvre. Eighteenth Century.

cannot ask of wood carving the severity and simplicity
which are demanded by the intractability, weight, and
hardness of stone. We could not say that the Fall of
Man has been seriously conceived in this pulpit, or that
clouds and drapery hangings are a proper matter even for
wood carving, and still the ingenuity and thought with
which the subject has been wrought out stand for a great
deal.

Conceding much merit and interest to this work, we
shall also conclude from it and from its surroundings that
the pompous display of material wealth in art was a ruling
trait of the time. The
affected style and at-
titudes of the statues
on the adjacent col-
umns of the church are
characteristic for the
whole Renaissance
sculpture of the seven-
teenth century.

Finally we have an
illustration (Fig. 154)
to represent the ex-
istence of the artist,
viz., Bernini, who of
all men of his cen-
tury combined the
greatest genius and
talent with the most
pronounced display of

FIG. 158.—Statue of Louis XV., by Nicolas Coustou. Louvre.

the traits we have enumerated, over-wrought or compli-
cated subjects, the substitution of mechanical dexterity for
thought, and the exaltation of costly material at the ex-

pense of subject matter. Bernini was also a decorator and architect of distinction, the designer of the colonnade surrounding the large oval place in front of St. Peter's, of its interior colossal bronze shrine, and of many churches.

The whole later Renaissance was at its best in portrait sculpture, especially of busts. Both French and Italian sculptors were eminent in this specialty. Puget was the greatest French sculptor of this era, the age of Louis XIV., who himself employed Bernini in Paris while Puget was also active in Italy and at Rome.

As an illustration of the portrait sculpture of the late Renaissance and of the eighteenth century, I have chosen a statue of the French king, Louis XV., whose pose exhibits the theatrical quality characteristic of the time.

CHAPTER XXIX.

ACCORDING to our account so far, throughout this whole book, either of architecture, painting, or sculpture, it will appear that the earlier eighteenth century represents the foot of a hill whose gradual descent began about 1530.

We shall not, however, be entirely just to our subject without remarking that to the simile of decline, which has been used above, we must add one which indicates an ever widening expansion of Italian culture and of the original force and attainments of early modern Italian civilization; an expansion which would justify and explain a gradual loss of original quality and strength as far as exterior and borrowed forms of art are concerned. Such a simile may be found in those expanding circles of waves or ripples which we notice when a stone has been thrown into a pool of water. Corresponding to the suggestions of this simile, we find the civilization of Russia or of Scandinavia beginning to show more modern tendencies in the eighteenth century and that England and Prussia became the most powerful and active factors in its political history, as compared with an earlier political inferiority to the Netherlands, Spain, and France, which in their turn had been the superiors of seventeenth century Italy, although originally borrowers from her greatness. It is undoubtedly from this point of view that we must explain the great perfection of English painting in the eighteenth century; the time of Wilson in landscape, of Gainsborough and

FIG. 159.—Portrait of Col. Epes Sargent, by John Singleton Copley. Photographed for this work at the Columbian Exposition, by permission of Mrs. George H. Clements.

Reynolds, Lawrence and Romney in portraits, of Hogarth in caricature, of George Morland in farm scenes and the like, as compared with earlier English obscurity in the matter of great painters (p. 181). So again it is at the close of the eighteenth century that we find the dawning genius of early American painters, like Copley and Gilbert Stuart, again in dependence on an inspiration and style of earlier English origin. The revival of art in England belongs, however, to a time, that of the later eighteenth century, when northern Europe in general was beginning to assert its independence of Italian Renaissance influences in a way which I must now describe. The sketch of the later course of the history of art, after the middle of the eighteenth century, moves properly from the history of Renaissance sculpture as just concluded in my last chapter, because it was in sculpture that the art decadence of the early eighteenth century was most clearly visible, and because it was in the study of ancient Greek sculpture as contrasted with this decadence that modern art began its new career.

Sculpture had been the art in which decadence was most apparent because the picturesque and sentimental tastes of the later Renaissance were least adapted to its proper conditions of dignity and repose. Architecture was restrained by its dimensions and serious practical problems from sinning invariably as it did frequently, but we have given examples of its mistakes of profusion of ornament, and of lack of sense for construction (Fig. 51 and pp. 97-102).

We have also found that the seventeenth century produced its greatest school of painting in a country (Holland) whose religion, location, and history were most remote to that of Renaissance Italy. Still, Renaissance painting was the art which held to its best for the longest time and which never entirely sacrificed its greatness. Its ascendency and relative perfection as compared with later Renaissance architecture and sculpture are marked, and we should not be far from the heart of the matter in saying that the defects of these arts for the given time were largely due to a pictorial influence and tendency not befitting their necessary dignity.

If we should go still deeper in attempting to explain the gradual decline of art, it would be by saying that the intellectual inspiration of the Renaissance had exhausted its subject matter. Italy had risen from the study of Roman history and Latin literature to greatness, but in the middle of the eighteenth century Europe had subsisted on the fruits of Italian thought and energy for at least two hundred years. A new force and a new center of activity, new thoughts and new interests were needed.

In the history of governments we see how the system of early modern history had grown decrepit and weak, how the despotic monarchies of the eighteenth century had lost their former hold on popular favor and support. Just as the French Revolution at the close of the eighteenth century was an explosion of protest against a fossil stage of government, so the intellectual thought of Europe had its revival just preceding, which in fact resulted in this political explosion.

The turning point in the history of Renaissance and modern art is the revolution in taste caused by the revived study of Greek literature after 1750. We have seen that the Greek men of letters, driven into Italy by the Turkish conquest of the Byzantine Empire in the fifteenth century, spread and cultivated the study of Greek in Italy. But these studies were crippled by the social and political dis-

asters which came to notice in our account of Michael
Angelo (p. 223) and of the decline of the historic Renaissance (p. 37).

The older social aristocracies of Italy which had cultivated these studies were now ruined and dispersed. The
Catholic Church Reformation, which accompanied the
Protestant reform, took . alarm at the pagan and infidel
tendencies which the intellectual worship of paganism was
supposed to have caused, and it was in the Greek circles of
Italy that these tendencies had been manifest.

To the changed attitude of the Roman Church was
added a still more important cause—the natural tastes and
predispositions of the mass of Italians in favor of Latin,
and the ease with which they could learn it, through its
connection with their own tongue. To these various causes
we may attribute the decline in the estimation of the
Greek authors and the general indifference to them which
became the rule throughout Europe.

In spite of exceptions and some apparent contradictions,
Greek studies were mainly ignored in the seventeenth century and during the first half of the eighteenth century. At
this time there was only one university in Germany having
a professorship in Greek—the University of Göttingen.

The father of the Greek Revival, John Winckelmann,
who was in early life too poor to buy many books, had not
been able up to the time when he was thirty years old
even to borrow a copy of Sophocles. No edition of Plato
had been published in Europe at this time since the year
1602. No Greek authors had been published in Germany
for one hundred and fifty years. No school books for
the study of Greek were available when Winckelmann,
as schoolmaster at Seehausen, introduced the study of
Greek into his school. He was obliged to write out texts

for his scholars—these manuscripts are still in existence.

Leading French critics did not hesitate to ridicule the Greeks. One of them (Pérrault) compared Homer to the ballads of the street singers of Paris. Voltaire declared the Æneid to be superior to all the Greek authors taken together. Such were the general results of the attitude of the later Renaissance and of its enthusiasm for Roman antiquity and Latin literature. The neglect of Greek may possibly be less apparent in England, which country was most exterior to the influence of the later Renaissance and its prejudices, but Macaulay has contributed valuable hints on this matter of English neglect of Greek, in his essay on Addison.*

All this was changed by the epoch-making life of Winckelmann, who rose from a position of extreme poverty and obscurity to be the leading antiquarian and art critic of Europe. It was not till the year 1755, when he began his residence at Rome that any indication of this distinction became apparent, and he had already reached the age of thirty-eight. In the following thirteen years he did work which revolutionized the taste and art of Europe.

It was a time before the foundation of the later museums of the North and when the antique statues were almost exclusively confined to Rome. Here they were supposed to be works representing Roman history and civilization and explaining Latin literature. Strange as it may seem, Winckelmann's announcement of the existence of a Greek art as perpetuated by Roman copies was a complete revelation to his age, which was quite ignorant of the originals subsequently brought from Greece to northern

* The most important authority is the German author Carl Justi, "Das Leben Winckelmannes." For the ultimate Renaissance neglect of Greek studies in Italy, see also Jacob Burckhardt's "Civilization of the Renaissance in Italy."

Europe like the Parthenon marbles of the British Museum.

This announcement was not made suddenly or ostentatiously, but by a series of reversals of interpretations of the ancient statues in Rome, which had been given interpretations based on Latin literature and Roman history.

To this reversal of the older Italian interpretations of the statues Winckelmann added a new point of view in their criticism. In the early Renaissance it had been the realistic study of natural form which had interested the Italian.

Fig. 160.—Ganymede, by Thorwaldsen.
Copenhagen.

The ancient statues which the Italian especially admired were those few in which the anatomic details were most exaggerated. These were shown by Winckelmann to be works of the Greek decadence.

On the other hand, the taste of the eighteenth and seventeenth centuries for exaggerated, ostentatious, and theatrical art had entirely overlooked the virtues of repose and simplicity in the works which Winckelmann now proved to be simply Roman copies of lost Greek originals. Still farther he specified the various historic styles within the limits of Greek art and gave their proper rank to the conceptions of the fifth century before Christ, the period of Phidias.

These points were first made known to the world in Winckelmann's History of Art, published in 1764. The effect of this publication was electrical. In proving the Roman statues to be copies of Greek originals a new conception was involved of the general origin of Roman civilization and Latin literature. It was no longer possible to esteem the Latin authors above the Greeks when these were seen to have been the models followed by the Romans.

Thus the study of ancient sculpture reacted on the study of ancient literature. The Greek authors suddenly became fashionable. The impulse thus given by Winckelmann was aided by Lessing, who published, in 1766, his "Essay on Laocoön," critically

FIG. 161—Detail from the Perseus, by Canova. Vatican. Rome.

establishing the superiority of Homer and lowering the position which had been awarded the French critics and dramatists of the eighteenth century.

Now came the influence, first on Germany, and then on all Europe, of the German poets Goethe and Schiller and their followers, who stood on the platform established by Winckelmann and Lessing and owed their own greatness to the inspiration drawn from the Greek literature. The whole of

Europe was now permeated by a new antique fever resembling the Renaissance and known as the Greek Revival, or Philhellenic movement.

The influence on modern art was phenomenal. Even in clocks and furniture no style of design was now tolerated but imitation of the Greeks. The Renaissance style of architecture was combated by another which appealed to the constructional principles of the Greek temples as contrasted with the ornamental and unstructural use of Greek forms borrowed by Italy from the Romans.

FIG. 162.—The Angel of Death. Detail of the Tomb of Clement XIII. in St. Peter's. By Canova.

In practice the two styles were, however, frequently amalgamated, for not all architects were capable of sharing the literary enthusiasms of the new movement. Still a pronounced simplicity in architectural forms was a feature of the Greek Revival, and the Greek porticoes and colonnades were everywhere copied and applied to modern buildings. Many were even made in direct imitation of the shape of the Greek temples, as numerous churches and public buildings still attest.

By the last quarter of the eighteenth century the Greek Revival was the most pronounced feature of European history. Even politics showed this influence and the revolutions in both France and America were largely inspired by an ideal of republican institutions drawn from the study of Plutarch's " Lives," which was the most popular book of the time. In ladies' dress the style now known as that of the " Directory," and represented by the short-waisted ladies' dress of the time of the American Revolution, came into vogue as a copy of Greek simplicity. In music the subjects of Gluck's Operas are a reminder of the same enthusiasms.

In statuary the same movement was equally visible. The theatrical and sentimental style of sculpture was abandoned and a new one was founded, based upon an external imitation of Greek art. In this taste the Italian Canova and the Dane Thorwaldsen, long resident at Rome, were the first and most prominent lights, and the imitation of the Greeks in sculpture is only in recent years beginning to yield to a more original and truly modern style. In this recent movement the sculptors of the United States are among the foremost, and taken in mass have probably achieved the best results of modern sculpture.

In painting the classical spirit also showed itself, and its first leading light was the Frenchman David, a contemporary of the French Revolution and of the times of Bonaparte. In this art, however, the first and most obvious result of the Greek Revival was a return of appreciation for the period of Raphael, whose virtues of repose and simplicity were parallel in painting to the same qualities of the Greek sculpture. In other words, the results in painting were more apparent in a changed standard of appreciation toward old Italian art than in a new style of modern painting.

CHAPTER XXX.

THE period of the Greek Revival, which continued in full vigor through the first quarter of the nineteenth century, was subsequently antagonized and partially displaced by a new movement of historic studies and literary tastes which turned once more to the appreciation of the Middle Age.

The prejudice against the art and culture of the Middle Age, which had coined the word "Gothic," was of Italian origin—as we have seen (p. 56). No stronger illustration could be given of the duration and ascendency throughout Europe of the Renaissance than the contempt for the old cathedrals, which lasted till the close of the eighteenth century.

The Greek Revival continued to hold this attitude of indifference and contempt, but it developed, as we have seen, a new school of German literature. In the great revolt of Germany against the ascendency of Bonaparte, which marked the first fifteen years of the nineteenth century, a feeling of national patriotism, cultivated by this literature and by this revolt, began to rise superior to the jealousies which had so far divided and estranged the petty states and principalities of Germany. Proud of their own great authors, musical composers, and men of science, the Germans turned to the study of their own past, and the greatness of this past was found to lie in the period when all Europe had been Germanized and conquered by Germans—when the feudal system had developed from Ger-

manic institutions; when Charlemagne had reconsolidated
Europe; when the Saxon, Franconian, and Hohenstaufen
emperors had been the leaders of their day; when the
League of the Hansa had created the commerce and
fostered the industries of northeastern Europe.

Thus the German became the first historic student of the
long despised period of the Middle Ages. The Greek
Revival had given him the consciousness of national existence through its influence on the creation of a national
literature. This literature then turned the thoughts of the
people to the study of their own history and their own
past.

The Gothic Revival was thus as a literary and historic
study gathering force in Germany through the first quarter
of the nineteenth century. Then it burst its national
barriers and spread through Europe. France and England, no less than Germany, turned attention to their own
medieval past. This movement is especially represented
for England by the romances of Sir Walter Scott, which
were the first works of English literature to draw attention
to the Middle Ages.

All this reacted on the exterior forms of modern art.
The cathedrals which the "Spectator" of Addison had
held up to ridicule, which the cultivated Evelyn had stigma-
tized as "only Gothic,"* which Winckelmann had considered unworthy of notice, and which even Lessing had
neglected, were now exalted at the expense of Roman
buildings and Greek temples as the models of all modern
architectural forms.

Meantime both Renaissance and Greek details continued
to hold their own in that traditional use which did not
readily yield to the new crusade of the historians and men

* See Evelyn's "Diary," time of Charles II. of England.

of letters.   The field of church architecture, at least, however, was fully conquered by the Gothic.   It would be
difficult to specify a church built in Europe or America
about or after 1850 which did not exhibit the Gothic style.

To this style succeeded copies of the Romanesque* and
Italian Gothic.   The Romanesque, as being earlier than
Gothic, and the Italian
Gothic, as more re-
mote from the first
modern students of
the Gothic in northern
Europe, had at first at-
tracted less attention.
As the knowledge of
medieval architecture
became wider and more
general, these remoter
or earlier styles were
also drawn upon as
models for copy.

Meantime the at-
tention of historic
students and critics
veered from an en-
thusiastic admiration
for the beauty of the old monuments to a critical appreciation of their common sense in construction.   This appreciation again naturally called attention to the new problems
of construction in modern architecture and the inadvisa-
bility of thrusting a common-sense ancient mode of
construction on a modern building with different require-
ments and character.

FIG. 163.—Houses of Parliament, London.
By Barry.   Gothic Revival.

---

* Compare "Roman and Medieval Art."

This new point of view was much assisted by the Decorative Art movement which gradually developed in England after the Crystal Palace Exposition of 1851. The leading idea of this movement under its original leaders was to make ornament the emphasis and exponent of construction. This idea had again been evolved principally from the study of the Gothic, but was seen to be equally supported by the principles of the original Greek monuments.

Whereas the Greek Revival had insisted on the constructional use of *Greek* forms as against the Renaissance, but had continued to regard the classic details as the exclusive models of imitation, the ultimate outcome of the Gothic revival was the tendency to abjure any use of historic style of any period which did not harmonize with the common-sense uses and purposes of the modern time. But it was difficult and impossible to create a modern style out of nothing, with no antecedents and no traditions. Such an out-and-out original creation was never known to history where evolution has always been the mode of change.

In this dilemma between the theories of the professors, who taught that constructive truth was the only standard of taste as applied to form, and the habits of the modern architect, who had never since 1500 done anything but borrow his details from historic styles—the "Italian Gothic" and "Romanesque," for the time being, offered an obvious compromise. Both were styles in which the effects of masonry surface had been undisturbed by projecting buttresses or projecting "engaged columns." As far as masonry construction was concerned, here were styles, so-called, which were adapted to any modern building. The decorative details were medieval, instead of classic—this was a matter of indifference or of personal taste as long as they were not allowed to determine constructional forms.

In modern "Italian Gothic" and "Romanesque" we have had a compromise between the general dependence of modern architecture on past models, and the reaction against the purely literary and archæologic imitation of Gothic cathedrals, or the expensive and generally worn-out forms of the traditional Renaissance, or the expensive and frequently unnecessary colonnades of the Greeks.

FIG. 164.—Courthouse and Jail of Pittsburg. By H. H. Richardson. Romanesque Revival.

Side by side with this movement and slightly later in time came the so-called "Queen Anne" and "Colonial" styles, which were especially applied to country houses and suburban residences, whereas the Italian Gothic and Romanesque, as exclusively masonry and not timber styles, had been more confined to the cities.

In these last revivals we see partly the swinging back of the pendulum toward the Renaissance under which "Colonial" and "Queen Anne" must be included, but Renaissance of a simpler class, less pretentious, and with details of greater beauty than had survived in the purely traditional forms of brownstone fronts and American government buildings. Recurrence to our remarks on Dutch buildings of the seventeenth century will assist this explanation (p. 104). Otherwise, "Queen Anne" and "Colonial" may be explained as an appreciation of fashion for the picturesque and common-sense construction of the given periods, and both styles, so-called, as well as Italian Gothic and Romanesque, have been convenient cloaks for architects intent on solving modern problems in their own way—without caring to make martyrs of themselves by explaining to their patrons that it makes very little difference what old name may be given a modern building. In all these varying currents and eddies of the hour, we can still see in our own country the steady movement of a great nation toward the assertion of its own needs and character and the realization of its own opportunities.

CHAPTER XXXI.

SCULPTURE IN THE NINETEENTH CENTURY.

Of all arts of the nineteenth century, sculpture is the one which longest retained and exhibited the influences dating from the later half of the eighteenth century. Only in quite recent years has it begun to shake off the imitative quality which the Greek Revival had stamped upon it. The reasons for this are obvious. The pre-eminence of the Greeks in sculpture is so unquestioned and the fame of their works so great, that all later art must bow before it. When the influences of literary fashion and historic interest were added to the weight of the technical superiority and artistic value, the inevitable result, for the time being, was imitation. This imitation being the rage in general, the art in which the Greek was most admired experienced the result most

Fig. 165.—Teucer, by Hamo Thornycroft. (See Fig. 169.) Photographed, by permission, for this work, at the Columbian Exposition.

sensibly. Thus, to the period of Thorwaldsen, the imitation of Greek sculpture appeared to be a necessary consequence of its admitted superiority. The modern copyists overlooked, however, the point that the Greeks had not reached their greatness in sculpture by studying statues. Although they had idealized nature, they had always based their art upon it. One defect of the Greek Revival statuary was, consequently, a cold and formal quality—resulting from the habit of studying statues as distinct from the study of living nature. It should be added, too, that little was known in the late eighteenth and early nineteenth centuries of the vigor and

Fig. 166.—Bronze Equestrian Statue of Frederick the Great. By Rauch. Berlin (1851).

life of original Greek art. The models followed had been mainly those of the Roman period. It was not till the year 1816 that the British government agreed to purchase the Elgin Marbles, although they had then been in London for nine years.

After the time of Canova the Italian sculpture sank into insignificance. The Greek School was meantime headed for northern Europe by the names of the English John Gibson and the German Dannecker. In both these artists

we notice the deficiency of vigorous modeling peculiar to
the imitative Greek School, Canova and Thorwaldsen included.   The lack of differentiation in execution between
details and bodily forms was also a weakness—a weakness
never found in the antique art which was supposed to be
imitated.   An over-delicate finish of surface and refinement in representing textures have not been confined to the
Greek Revival, and still impair the value of a great deal
of more recent sculpture, but this deficiency appears most
objectionable when the pretense of idealism is suggested.
We must concede, on the other hand, to the modern Greek
Revival, nobility of purpose, refinement of thought, and an
absence of those glaring offenses to good taste in the way
of extravagant and pretentious poses and conceptions which

had been the almost
universal rule in late
Renaissance sculpture.
This point will appear
if the reader will com-
pare its illustrations
with those for Thor-
waldsen and Canova.

On the whole, the
German sculptors
Rauch and Kiss repre-
sent the highest level
of success for the first

Fig. 167.—Andromeda. Design for the Gates of
Hell. (Dante's Inferno.) By Rodin. Photographed, by permission, for this work,
at the Columbian Exposition.

half of the nineteenth century.   Both of these artists had
risen to independent mastery of form and independent representation of it.   Rauch's great monument of Frederick
the Great in Berlin is the finest of its kind in Europe.   The
Amazon, by Kiss, fronting the entrance to the Berlin
Museum, is one of the most powerful of modern works.

In more recent years the credit of shaking off the trammels of imitative Grecianizing sculpture belongs especially to the artists of France, and in this movement the influence of the early Renaissance, as nearer to our own time than the Greek in its attitude toward nature, had no small share. Among these French artists we may mention Carpeaux,

FIG. 168.—Cast of a Lion, by Barye. Trocadero Museum, Paris.

Falguière, and the isolated and powerful genius of Rodin. For uncompromising realism, sense of character, and powerful and bold summary of the essentials of form (as distinct from minute and over-anxious specializing of details) the French sculptor Barye has no superior in modern art. His devotion to the field of animal sculpture may be considered a limitation when the element of thought in art is given its place, but this colossal genius was able to find a field in animals which did not expose him to the prejudices and preoccupations of modern amateurs so long accustomed in figure design to the imitation of classic art. The name of Cain stands only second to Barye in the same field.

Among the most powerful and original English sculptors of the new school are Hamo Thornycroft and Sir Frederick Leighton. Sir Frederick Leighton's statue of "The Sluggard," exhibited at the Columbian Exposition, must have been a revelation to all who have known him simply as a painter. It ranks among the very first works of modern sculpture in the last four centuries. The same must be said of Thornycroft's "Teucer," which is one of the treasures of the Art Institute of Chicago, and one of the finest works of foreign sculpture owned in this country. It is not, however, advisable to enlarge the catalogue of works even at the risk of omitting those of men of genius. The main point is to state the tendency which the last twenty-five years have everywhere exhibited—the tendency to learn principles of execution from the Greeks, without borrowing their subjects or imitating the exterior appearance of their art. Modern art for moderns, is the watchword at last.

To this tendency the younger sculptors of America have been especially influenced by the teachings of the best French masters, and under the inspiration of this tuition have risen to a point of greatness where they have become their worthy rivals. In fact, when we distinguish the technical ability in which the French have been especially eminent, from the thought, conception, and purpose of the art, the palm may even now be awarded to American sculpture. In this distinction we do not wish to imply any technical inferiority in the American School, but rather to refrain from asserting for it a superiority of simple execution and to claim for it by contrast the superiority of a more genuine, original spirit, and of a fresher and purer inspiration. We can only say that no opportunity has ever been offered modern sculpture like that assigned it in the statuary for the buildings and grounds at the Columbian Exposition, and that American artists rose to the occasion and were equal to it. Nor should we overlook in this assertion the foreign birth of some of the gentlemen who bore away great honors, or appear to be ignorant of their share in the great success achieved. We can at least lay claim to the honor that they have made America their second and adopted home, and that their genius found its recognition here.

In the earlier years of this century and the earlier days of American sculpture, the name of Hiram Powers long held sway as the leading one. To-day we must confess that our interest in him is historical and that he is the weakest of all Greek imitators who have achieved a name. That he was the first of American sculptors to make a name must be conceded. His ability did not go farther than that

FIG. 169.—Teucer, by Hamo Thornycroft. Property of the Art Institute of Chicago. Photographed, by permission, for this work, at the Columbian Exposition.

of making a weak imitation of the Medici Venus, with deviations of pose and attitude sufficient to allow of a new baptism. His "Greek Slave," known in several copies, had a world-wide reputation about the middle of this century—when critics were less exacting than they are to-day. The names of Crawford (bronze doors of the Capitol at Washington) and Palmer, possibly less quoted than Hiram Powers, will stand far higher. In the days following the Civil War the statuette groups of John Rogers had a popularity which they have not yet entirely lost. They do not claim to be more than pictures in clay, but, making all concessions to the humility of size and purpose, we must still refrain from awarding praise to these groups. Deficiency in dignity should not alone condemn a small and unpretentious group or statuette, but these works are a dangerous concession to the taste which looks to the imitation of textures and the representation of anecdotes and incidents by plastic art. The statue of Lincoln, by Rogers, seen at the Columbian Exposition, is a serious and important work of the first class. To judge from this statue, his little groups have been one of those concessions of the breadwinner to popular taste, of which modern art is, unhappily, so full. It is useless to criticise an artist in such matters, where only the public is to blame.

Toward the close of the third quarter of our century the names of Launt Thompson and J. Q. A. Ward were probably the most important. The dignity, reserve, and simplicity of Thompson's work have been universally recognized. His portrait statues of Yale, at New Haven, and of Bonaparte, in the Museum of New York, will long hold their own. John Quincy Ward is the great father of recent American sculpture, and his bronze statue of Henry Ward Beecher, in Brooklyn, proves that his talent is still young in these later years. All of Ward's works are careful, exact, and conscientious studies. His Beecher is an inspiration.

We come then to the latest, best, and youngest gener- .

Fig. 170.—Bronze Group. Charles Dickens and Little Nell, by F. Edwin Elwell. Published by permission of the Artist.

ation of American sculptors, headed by Augustus St. Gaudens, Olin Warner, and Daniel C. French, names of such distinction that to praise them is superfluous and to criticise them impossible or impertinent. What younger artists will wrench their laurels from them is uncertain, but Potter, Partridge, and Boyle, Taft, Rubisso, and Mac-Monnies, Dalin, Proctor, and Kemeys, Adams, Kitson, and Donoghue, Tilden, Wesselhœft, Bartlett, Grafly, and Elwell are among the number of their rivals.

Fig. 171.—Bronze Statue of Henry Ward Beecher, Brooklyn. By J. Q. A. Ward.

Of all modern portrait statues of authors the "Dickens and Little Nell" of Mr. Edwin F. Elwell appears to me the most inspired. The thought of connecting an author with his favorite creation, of calling to life the phantom of the brain, of showing at once the author and his work in spiritual sympathy and union is an original and beautiful idea. Mr. Elwell's colossal Hancock, designed for the battlefield of Gettysburg, is one of the most important equestrian monuments of modern history.

Among the portrait statues of American Colonial heroes and statesmen there is surely none to rival the Hamilton of Wm. Ordway Partridge, in Brooklyn. As the ideal of an

FIG. 172.—Bronze Statue of Hamilton, Brooklyn. By William Ordway Partridge.
Published by permission of the Artist.

orator it appears to me the most successful work in modern
art.   It is the great fortune of Mr. Partridge to have a
practical knowledge of the art of the dramatist and of
elocution.   The combination in his Hamilton of statuesque
reserve with the suggestion of the spirited effort of a great
spokesman is a marvelous success.   The Shakespeare of
Mr. Partridge, in Lincoln Park, Chicago, is a refined and
dignified work of masterly detail.

In the preparations for the Columbian Exposition the su-

Fig. 173.—Landscape Group, by E. C. Potter and Daniel C. French.
Columbian Exposition.

preme task was assigned to Mr. Daniel C. French—a colossal statue of the "Republic."   The failure would have been
colossal, the success must be equally rated.   With every
increase of dimension in statuary its problem becomes
more difficult.   To say that this problem was solved with
beauty, with originality, with simplicity, and with dignity,

is saying what no one can deny. For the given place and given architectural surroundings to which the equally balanced and equally uplifted arms exactly corresponded, this has proved the most successful colossal work of modern sculpture. Its most obvious rivals would be the "Liberty" of New York harbor, the "Bavaria" in Munich, by Schwanthaler, and the "Hermann's Denkmal,"

FIG. 174.—Statue of the Republic. By Daniel C. French.

or monument of Arminius, near Detmold in Germany, and none of these can be called its equal. Mr. French's relief for the tomb of a

FIG. 175.—Sea Horses. Detail from the Fountain by MacMonnies. Columbian Exposition.

sculptor, called "The Angel of Death and the Sculptor," was exhibited in the Art Palace at the Columbian Exposition. Since the tomb reliefs of ancient Athens the works are few indeed which could compare with it.

For the statuary groups of the Court of Honor, Mr. French and Mr. Potter have already received a trib-

ute of appreciation to which I can only add my own.   No
similar works of modern history are deserving of equal place,
and I can see no reason for suggesting that antiquity sur-

FIG. 176.—Mounted Indian, by Proctor. Facing the Transportation
Building, Columbian Exposition.

passed them.   It should be added that their material, although perishable, was contributory to this success.   The
weakness of modern sculpture lies in its lack of constant
practice with the chisel.   The manual labor of cutting the
block of marble has been so constantly assigned to subordinate workmen that the mastery of chisel technique is more
or less wanting to the modern sculptor.   It is when his own
model can be directly transferred to cast in a material like
"staff," or actually worked up in this material, whose

rough surface is favorable to large effects, that the genius of the modern artist best stands comparison with his rivals of antiquity.

In the application of statuary to architectural decoration the use of this material again allowed the artists of the Columbian Exposition to achieve a scale and amount of decoration hitherto unknown, at least since the time of the Romans, and again they were equal to the occasion. No works of the kind in modern art can be compared with those achieved by Mr. Carl Bitter and Mr. Martiny for the Ad-

FIG. 177.—Aerial Navigation, by John J. Boyle. Transportation Building, Columbian Exposition.

ministration and Agricultural buildings. The works of Mr. Boyle and Mr. Taft on the Transportation and Horticultural buildings are also deserving of great praise. The

Indian of Mr. Boyle, in Lincoln Park, Chicago, is his great
masterpiece.

In our account of the artistic triumphs of the Columbian
Exposition we have also to mention the masterly animal
sculptures of Mr. Proctor and Mr. Kemeys with which the
grounds were filled. The Buffalo Hunt of Mr. Bush-Brown,
which was a central piece of the Art Palace, shows him a
finished master in the same specialty. Mention of the great fountain of the Court of Honor, by Frederick MacMonnies, may close our effort to do justice to the almost inexhaustible list of masterpieces offered by the Columbian Exposition. The sea-horses surrounding its "triumphal barge" have never had their superiors.

Fig. 178.—Bronze Statue of Abraham Lincoln. By Augustus St. Gaudens. Lincoln Park, Chicago.

The most generally quoted masterpiece of Augustus St. Gaudens is the bronze statue of Abraham Lincoln in Lincoln Park, Chicago.

Its uncompromising and honest realism appeals to every
eye. On the other hand, the reliefs of this master are of
ideal and classic beauty. In fact it is hard to see where
parallels can be found for the recent relief work of several
American sculptors short of the fifteenth century. Several

of them are unquestionably superior to Thorwaldsen, as being of fresher and more genuine spirit and not deficient in equal beauty of composition.

In the application of color to works of sculpture, Mr. Herbert Adams is foremost among American artists, as known to me. Since the time of John Gibson no important work has previously been done in this direction. That of Mr. Adams is tender and beautiful. In face of such work the prejudice against colored sculpture is destined to disappear rapidly.

CHAPTER XXXII.

ENGLISH AND FRENCH PAINTING.

Eighteenth and Nineteenth Centuries.

THE painting of the late eighteenth and early nineteenth centuries did not for Europe at large rise above a rather weak reflex of the contemporary movement in literature and in the sister arts. It threw off the last vestige of eighteenth century traits, but did not rise above negative virtues in the main. It was praiseworthy rather for what it did not do than for what it did do. Its great progress was that it had learned to reverence the best Italians, rather than the worst—but the very greatness and unapproachable excellence of the newly admired and greatest Old Masters exercised for the time a crippling influence on its efforts. It could not resurrect the Italian art, and it could not assimilate it to modern uses. Modern painting was appreciative but not creative.

The most important revival in the art of figure composition was that of the German Cornelius (frescoes in Munich) and of Kaulbach (frescoes in the Berlin Museum), but neither these artists nor any of their contemporary countrymen were able to reach a corresponding success in warmth or harmony of color. The later artists of Munich, headed by Piloty, were the first among Germans to reach relative success in color. These again were followed by the first and only German who has approached the gorgeous and sumptuous color of the old Venetians, the Viennese Hans Makart.

In France the elegant court life of the eighteenth century had furnished interesting subjects for the brush of Watteau. At its close Greuze had represented a new school of realism, in which one side of the social revolution was reflected,

Fig. 179. - Boy Fighting, by Gainsborough. Photographed for this work, by permission of the owner, Mr. Henry T. Chapman, of Brooklyn.

while David represented the classical tendencies of the same period. The portraits of Gérard have handed down to us many of the great characters of this time in pictures worthy of them. Gros and Géricault were later contemporaries of

David, in whom a vigorous sense of reality asserts itself, and to these again succeeded Eugene Delacroix, as the artist of passion and of power.

Meantime a colder classical French School was apparently in the ascendant, clinging to tradition and fearing to concede the greatness of the true men of genius silently work-

FIG. 180.—Landscape, by Diaz. Photographed for this work, by permission of the owner, Mr. Henry T. Chapman, of Brooklyn.

ing in obscurity.   To these, then more obscure French painters of the years 1825–1850 and later, posterity has now rendered full justice, and the names of Corot, of Millet, of Decamps, of Michel, and of Rousseau are on every lip.

Of the same time, and following the same tendencies, are Dupré, Troyon, Monticelli, and Diaz.   The special bias and excellence of this great French School, dating from the second quarter of the nineteenth century, and the greatest of recent times, are best explained by turning back to Eng-

FIG. 181.—Peasant Woman, by Millet. Photographed for this work, by permission of the owner, Mr. Henry T. Chapman, of Brooklyn.

land in the eighteenth century, where we shall find the connecting link between the older art of the Continent and the greatest modern art of France.

We have seen that England had no painters of renown
until the eighteenth century, and that her two most quoted
painters of preceding time were foreigners (p. 181). To
her great artists of the eighteenth century, on the other
hand, Continental Europe can offer no contemporary rivals;
a fact which we can place in proper perspective of history

FIG. 182.—Landscape, by Corot. Photographed for this work, by permission of
the owner, Mr. Henry T. Chapman, of Brooklyn.

only by understanding the backwardness of English culture
before this time, and also the way in which a movement of intellect and art passes from one country to another; each fire,
as it expires, lighting a new spark for perpetuation elsewhere
of the same eternal principles of beauty, of color, and of form.

The worthy perpetuators of the older traditions of European painting were the English artists, Wilson, Morland, Reynolds, Gainsborough, and their school. Through these men and their successors, of whom Constable and Etty were closest in method to their great predecessors, these traditions were handed over to the French School, headed by Rousseau, about 1830, at a time when English fashions were ascendant in France and when these English artists were highly valued and appreciated there. Intermediate in time, between the eighteenth century English and the 1830 School of France, stand the English landscape artists, Constable and Turner. It was the pictures and personal influence of Constable which most powerfully and directly influenced the French.

It is more especially in landscapes that the continuity of influence between the art of Constable and of Rousseau is seen, and in both painters we find the same disposition to look at things in their effects and masses rather than in their details.

To appreciate the greatness of these men of genius, we must remember that some of the most elementary principles are frequently overlooked by those inferior landscapists and their admirers, whose numbers have been large in our century. It is often forgotten that a picture is several or many thousand times smaller than the nature which it includes. To reduce each dimension and object of nature to the proportionate fractional size, and to show it in the same distinctness in which it might *possibly*, and when separately examined, be seen in nature, is the effort of the inferior landscapist. In this effort such an artist forgets that *simultaneous* concentration of the eye on a multitude of separate details is not possible in actual vision.

Persuasion, belief, and knowledge that these separate

details have a distinct existence are present to us, but we *see* a tree and not the leaves, a lake, but not its individual waves, a human being, but not the various portions of the raiment, that is when one glance takes in the whole. The possibility exists, because time allows it, of uniting on a

FIG. 183.—Landscape, by Claude Lorrain. Photographed for this work by permission of the Owner, Mr. Henry T. Chapman, of Brooklyn.

canvas surface a series of minimized *replicas* of the parts which make up a whole in nature. The possibility exists, because the eye can take in the canvas in a few glances or in one, that the eye may take in the parts which make the picture so as to affect the mind with the belief that it sees the whole as it is seen in nature. But the person who knows how he really sees will never be willing to call a work of art in landscape anything which minimizes and emphasizes all its details in fractional proportion and reduction.

In actuality our eye wanders from instant to instant in order to include a whole. The artist who presents this whole as though the eye were fixed on one point is bound, logically, to present all others in the vague way best described by the appearance of an object we are *not* looking at, as included in the outer circle of view and as it strikes the outer corner of the eye on the extreme edge of vision. But no artist

FIG. 184.—Landscape, by Homer Martin. Photographed for this work at the Columbian Exposition, by permission of the Artist.

could attempt this feat; therefore the problem of the landscape painter is to present in one view the imaginary result of a series of glances and *no one* of these will have included a microscopic catalogue of details.

This effort to describe the philosophy of a Claude, a Constable, or a Corot, leaves out the element of color, as being mainly undebatable on paper or at least undebatable without two definite examples of color in mind, one better and one worse.

We may again take refuge in this difficulty by describing an inferior art and an inferior taste in color as that which prefers things in pictures more highly colored, or "sweetened," than they actually are. For instance, we might

FIG. 185.—Maine Coast in Winter. Winslow Homer. Photographed for this work at the Columbian Exposition, by permission of the Artist and Owner.

like to see bootblacks with rosy cheeks or clean faces, but we rarely do in nature, although they more frequently so appear in pictures. One greatness of Millet is that he does not over-color or highly color his peasant. A rough skin and a rough dress cannot be represented by clear or bright colors.

The sin of the commonplace painter is dressing up in
bright hues and tints an imaginary picture of rose-colored
things or people. It does not follow that a color not
actually seen in nature is not admissible in a painting. The
colors of nature never can be and never are reproduced in
a painting either in mass or in details. In details it would
be absurd to attempt it, for reasons already given. In
mass the effort is simply beyond possibility when we are
speaking of absolute actualities. What the great painter
does with his colors is to throw us into the state of mind or
sentiment which the sight of nature produces on us, and
here it is that the affinities of temperament, which are
largely affected by the same colors in the same way, come
in play in our preference for one colorist over another. It
is at this point that the question of the "low-toned picture"
presents itself. Although there are marked distinctions on
this head among the French artists we have named, the
"low tone" is a general trait of their work.

The "low-toned picture" appeals to a certain temperament. This temperament is the temperament of Rembrandt, of Ribot, or of Decamps, or of the American
Albert Ryder. This temperament prefers a certain mystery of effect, a picture to which one can return without
having seen the whole of it the first time it has been looked
at. The painting of nature which lasts is the painting in
which nature is not revealed too suddenly or too entirely.

In other words, the mystery of nature, which *in* nature
may lie in its magnitude, in its unfathomable space or
incomputable variety or in our sense that we have seen it
differently yesterday and shall again see it differently to-
morrow, or the mystery of character or of an event or
episode whose causes are unknown, uncomprehended or
not thought out—all this may be suggested by the "low-

toned picture" of the given subject. Being a piece of canvas taken in by one glance, on which the same lines and colors lie forever, the picture can only suggest the element of the unknown or the infinite by this device.

In all these points which I have tried to suggest as virtues of the greatest French artists of the nineteenth century or of the English School of the eighteenth century, we have applications of principles which are found as far back as Da Vinci, and which were never subsequently abandoned by the great painters of history. In such points lies the supreme excellence of the Old Masters, when they are considered as painters rather than as historic illustrations of general historic facts.

It is interesting to feel that between periods as distinct as the nineteenth century and the sixteenth, there is still a bond in the methods of the great artists, wide apart as is their mission and historic place. In fact, when we consider the deficiencies of patronage, of immediate appreciation, and of adequate reward which the greatest modern artists have labored under, their success and worth cannot be rated below that of their more fortunate brethren of the past—more fortunate as regards public support, an assured livelihood, and a subject matter which was ready-made and already at hand.

In what I have said of the philosophy of vision, I have so far mainly confined myself to landscape because it is a class of subject in which the enormous disparity of size between nature and copy is obvious, and in which the distinction between the infinite variety of nature and the amount of that infinitude which can be suggested by a copy is also obvious. It is easiest to show and feel for landscape that some choice has to be made as to what shall be attempted, easiest to show and feel for landscape that the effect of the whole is what must be attempted, and easiest to show and feel that this can be done only by presenting an object in mass or by presenting objects in masses, because the dimensions of the work of art are so greatly minimized as compared with the nature represented.

From this point it is not difficult to move to another. Given the difficulty of relating art to this kind of nature, it is clear that a choice of a point of view in a picture must have much to do with its quality. The panoramic point of view is the one to be avoided; the picturesque, that is, the limited point of view, is the one to be sought. It also follows that atmosphere should be used for contrast, and not for the most important feature of the picture. It is according to these principles, and on account of them, that Claude, Constable, Rousseau and his school, almost invariably show a foreground composition. Given a foreground composition, there again arises the problem of balance of opposition in objects, and of contrast in colors. Finally, the tone of the picture determines its standing. The gaudily colored picture tires and strains the eye, the low-toned picture rests it and also suggests more of the mystery of nature. Admitting the varieties of individual taste, of varieties of mood in the same taste, and the countless concessions which have to be made to individual genius and to the surrounding conditions, we may add one more and the most important trait.

The one first condition of all great painting is an honest interest in the work or the theme for its own sake, without reference to mercantile considerations. The mercantile element ruins a painting. The instant we detect in it the quality of being made to sell as opposed to the quality which shows that the artist would rather starve than concede one point of his convictions or even of his own individual

preference in the choice of a subject, we have touched the
first downward round of the ladder which leads to the cor-
ruption of art.

We will now return to the French School of 1825–1850

Fig. 186.—Labor, by J. F. Millet.

to observe that what has been said is not only an effort to
explain its greatness, but also to bring to the front the
numerous artists of our own country who are following the
same path.   Personal character is the only ultimate deter-
minant in art.   The facility of the hand is a matter of
practice.   It is the eye which controls the hand.   But the
power of vision is not the only thing in question here.
Even in landscape we see that the question of choice is all-
important.   In other subjects it is still more so.

Let us select the artist Millet as a personality, from which we may draw some lessons as to the choice of subject. Millet's well-known greatness consists in the devotion of his art to the life of the French peasantry—but observe that it is always the serious side of the peasant life that he has given us. It is not the peasant in holiday dress or making merry. The life of toil, the dignity, the pathos, and the humility of labor—that is the one theme of his pictures. From the recognized standing of Millet in French art we may determine, then, another point of view which may fix

FIG. 187.—A Great Gale. Winslow Homer. Photographed for this work at the Columbian Exposition, by permission of the Artist and Owner.

the position of the modern artist, viz., the point of view which concerns his purpose and his thought. It is easiest to illustrate this point of view when we are dealing with an intensely serious purpose, such as Millet forces us to recognize; but I should be far from wishing to confine the defi-

nition of serious art to that which is serious in subject. Let
us note, however, that the sphere of modern art includes
among its most important specialties that of the student of
daily life in its humble avocations, seeking to exalt and
glorify the lowly and the poor in spirit. Why should we
hesitate to name our own Winslow Homer as another
instance of this same tendency, and one of the greatest of
our day? The stamp of the genuine, true, and sturdy
spirit is never lacking in his pictures.

In the study of character and human nature in contem-

FIG. 188.—"Sailors, Take Warning." By Winslow Homer. Photographed for
this work at the Columbian Exposition, by permission of the Artist.

porary life, modern art has produced much that is great.
Both England and Germany have affected this class of subject more than the French, although without reaching a
similar average of technical value, especially in color. The
English artists of our day have been foremost among Euro-

pean painters in this class, and they have found their worthy rivals and occasional superiors in this country. Since the days of Wilkie, English art has reveled in the subjects of everyday life as an inexhaustible storehouse of humor, pathos, and interest—too often, however, with an

FIG. 189.—Greek Girls Playing at Ball.   Sir Frederick Leighton.

over-anxious nicety of details and without due reference to harmonies and tones of color.   Color has been the weak point of nineteenth century English, as well as of German, art.   The English School of our day cannot compare in this sense either with its own art of the eighteenth century or with the modern French.

To this rule the exceptions are mainly recent but conspicuous.   Sir Frederick Leighton is one of the most obvious, and Alma-Tadema another.   Both of these painters tend to the antiquarian, or the classic subject— Alma-Tadema with a painstaking minuteness of execution which leaves a somewhat frigid impression.   To the same

general class may be reckoned the excellent works of
Poynter. A far more powerful colorist than any of these
is John M. Swan, whose paintings at the Columbian Exposition were a striking revelation of the possibilities of modern and of English art.

FIG. 190.—Love and Death. By George F. Watts. From the English Loans at the Columbian Exposition.

In Burne-Jones we find another stamp of genius, imaginative like Leighton, but even more intent on effects of outline and the balance of figures; as a composer of designs, according to architectural schemes, basing very distinctly on the old Italians. The deceased Albert Moore had a similar bent and talent.

In George F. Watts we appreciate a greater idealist than Burne-Jones, or Rossetti—almost Shakespearean in his profound and touching allegories. The titles of his paintings are a key to their character, and the con-

ception never falls below the subject in suggestiveness and
poetic thought. "Love and Death" and "Love and Life"
were seen with other works, at the Columbian Exposition.
The latter has been presented by Mr. Watts "to the American nation." Briton Riviere is another Englishman hold-
ing an important place by the suggestive treatment of
subjects like "Daniel in the Lions' Den" or "Circe and the
Companions of Ulysses." In this latter picture the companions of Ulysses are turned to swine and crowding about

Fig. 191.—Reading from Homer. By Alma-Tadema. From the American
Loans at the Columbian Exposition.

the enchantress. On the whole, we must give a high place
to modern English art for its lofty efforts, nobility of
purpose, and moral worth. It has produced, however,
much that is commonplace, very little that will take high
rank in point of view of color, and no recent landscapes
that can be compared with the best French or the best
American. Many of its highly quoted names of the middle
period of the century are almost distressing revelations of
the backwardness of English art at that time, after their
works have been examined. Among these the animal

painter, Landseer, may be quoted as an instance; an artist
made widely known by engravings which are generally far
superior to his pictures.   A very fine Landseer in the

FIG. 192.—Sea Nymph.   By Burne-Jones.

possession of Mr. Jesse Haworth, near Manchester, is a
notable exception.

It seems worth while, in closing our notice of English
art, to return to Turner and the opening of the century for
a moment.   Turner was undoubtedly a master of supreme
genius.   It is only to be regretted that Mr. Ruskin's

enthusiastic perception of his genius should have led to an exaltation of the master, not to be regretted in itself, but tending to efface the greatness or superiority of other artists like Constable and Etty who were less fortunate in the eloquence of their spokesman or who had not any. As a colorist this painter can neither hold his own with his English predecessors nor with his French successors, and at least in Constable and in Monticelli he has found equals in his daring originality. The deficiency in color sense, of which the "Slave Ship" in the Boston Museum may serve as an example, was national for the given time, and should not be reckoned against Turner in view of his broad and masterly methods and poetic nature.

FIG. 193.—The Young Marsyas. By Elihu Vedder. Photographed for this work at the Columbian Exposition, by permission of the Artist and Owner.

CHAPTER XXXIII.

RECENT AMERICAN ART.

BEFORE turning to recent American art we shall do well to guard our position in the matter of methods as so far considered, aside from landscape, lest we appear to exclude from appreciation much meritorious art in small figure composition. The diminution of the field of view carries with itself logically the possibility of greater insistence on detail. There are even paintings where this detail may be conceded the main interest. The Dutch artist, Terburg, was especially famous for his satin dresses. Notice, now, two points. As regards the dimension of the figure, Terburg did not

Fig. 194.—Design for an Illustration of Browning's "Men and Women"—"Childe Roland to the Dark Tower Came." By John La Farge. Drawing dated 1860.

work in life-size; his figures may average perhaps a foot high. As regards the number of figures, his pictures limit them to two or three. Now the refinement of execution in a satin dress which makes the charm of a

FIG. 195.—Portrait, by J. S. Sargent. Photographed for this work at the Columbian Exposition, by permission of the Artist and Owner.

FIG. 196.—The Lair of the Sea Serpent. By Elihu Vedder. Property of the Boston Museum of Fine Arts. Photographed for this work at the Columbian Exposition, by permission of the Artist and Owner.

Terburg will create a nightmare of ugliness if applied to a life-size portrait. Compare the method of Mr. Sargent in life-size portraits (Fig. 195) for the execution which revives the methods of Velasquez or of Gainsborough. Conceive now of the method of Terburg applied not to one but to twenty or thirty life-size figures, and you produce the style of Brozik, whose colossal picture of Columbus before Ferdinand and Isabella is in the New York Museum. It would be unjust to stigmatize this one painter for a method which has ruined the art of hundreds of conscientious painters of our day. It is evident, then, that not only the dimensions of the original subject, but also the dimensions of the painting itself, outside of landscape art, are or should be controlling elements in the matter of method. In every landscape the actual dimensions of nature may be considered as almost without limit. In anecdotal figure composition on small sized panels and of limited actual extent in original nature, our point of view as to method, whether broad or more minute and literal, becomes largely one of personal preference. Where the eye can take in within a foot or so an anecdote or episode, the method, whether broad or minute in detail, is a matter of choice at the discretion of the painter, and in both methods good results may be obtained. The controlling question concerns not the method but the matter in such cases, and the ability of the artist within the limits of his chosen method. Where life-size figures or large paintings are in question there can be little question as to choice of methods as between the broad and the minutely detailed. The influence of Mr. William M. Chase, and of his followers, has in this sense been epoch-making for American art—especially for the design of the figure; and as against the belittling influences which English art of the middle of the century or

earlier had exercised on our own.   At an earlier day than
that of Mr. Chase, William M. Hunt was one of the few
missionaries of the new idea in American art.   One of its
very greatest exponents in all modern time has been, however, the deceased and long unappreciated George Fuller.
This artist was the Hawthorne of American painters, as
Wordsworth Thompson and Frederick James are among
its Fenimore Coopers.

Among American painters we should give a foremost

FIG. 197.—The Deserted Inn.   By Wordsworth Thompson.   Photographed for
this work at the Columbian Exposition, by permission of the Artist.

place to those who have faced that most national of all
subjects, when its interest for posterity is kept in view, the
American Indian. Mr. Brush's picture of the "The Sculptor
and the King" has even gone back to Aztec days, with rare
union of poetic thought and accurate historic suggestion,
and his "Indian and the Lily," also seen at the Columbian

Exposition, conveys, even by the mention of its subject
alone, a suggestion of its poetic and yet faithful picture of
the so-called American savage. The names of Farny and
Remington are familiar to all experts as other vivid por-
trayers of life on the borders of civilization; and R. A.

Fig. 108.—The Sculptor and the King. By George de Forest Brush. Photographed
for this work at the Columbian Exposition, by permission of the Artist.

Blakelock was also among the first to devote his great talents to these subjects.

In religious art, I noticed at the Columbian Exposition
the powerful "Christ and the Fishermen" of Mr. Du
Mond, and the noble and elevated paintings of La Farge
and of Poore. Mr. Thayer's "Virgin Enthroned" has
already achieved the national reputation which it deserves.

In this mention of individual names I am well aware
how far I am sinning by omissions—and by omissions
among the very greatest of our artists. One must publish

an entire catalogue in order to do justice to the genius in American art.

In the United States the place of the artist has been hitherto one of extreme difficulty and hard struggle. The natural tendency of a new country to look up to its older predecessors in art and science has led us to ignore or overlook the general equality and frequent superiority of our artists to those of the Old World, to which equality or superiority they have attained in the last twenty years. The art exhibits and sculptured decorative work of the

FIG. 199.—Christ and the Fishermen. By F. V. Du Mond. Photographed for this work at the Columbian Exposition, by permission of the Artist.

Columbian Exposition offered an excellent opportunity for the contrast of contemporary American art with that of Europe, and in this contrast we had no cause to shun the comparison. Among living artists it appears to me that our own take first rank for the following reasons:

In architectural sculpture and in open air sculpture the modern world has seen nothing to compare with the statuary at Chicago, and as illustrations of the possibilities of sculpture in architectural decoration there are no buildings of modern time which could rival the Agricultural Building and the Administration Building at the Columbian Exposition. In the application of statuary to park or landscape decoration and in its quality, the same superiority

FIG. 200.—"Got Him." By Henry F. Farny. Photographed for this work at the Columbian Exposition, by permission of the Artist.

may be asserted. The lesson that a work of art needs a definite destination, a definite purpose, and a definite relation to surroundings which demand it and call it into being, was well taught us by the Exposition. No opportunity like it had been offered in modern history.

In the painting exhibits of the Art Palace, American

landscape was so superior to that of England, which made
an especially fine representative exhibit, that even comparison was out of question.   To the French exhibit of landscape it was also far superior, in which statement it should
be remembered that the French exhibit was not representative to the same extent as that of other nations.

FIG. 201.—An Impromptu Affair in the Days of "The Code."   By Frederick
James.   Photographed for this work at the Columbian
Exposition, by permission of the Artist.

The American loans of contemporary French pictures
showed a finer quality than the French official display.
This is also significant for American taste.   Among the
living French artists represented by American loans only
Monet and Raffaelli could be mentioned as men of genius,
who surpassed in landscape their American competitors.
The works of Monet are extremely unequal and many of
them distinctly inferior to contemporary American; some of
them superior as works of daring genius to anything that

we have yet produced. The average superiority of American landscape to that of recent Germany and Italy is incontestable.

When we come to ideal or suggestive art of the lofty and ambitious type, I have no hesitation in placing Elihu Vedder as first among living moderns. He stands on surer ground in his choice of subjects, as being closer to average popular apprehension, than the Englishman George F. Watts. He is more profound than Leighton, not less suggestive and far more daring than Riviere, more practical and matter of fact than Burne-Jones, and there is no living Frenchman who can be named beside him in his peculiar field. Beside the name of Vedder, that of John La Farge must be mentioned as the worthy rival or superior of any living European artist of our day, Watts alone excepted, when the capacity of a poet and man of thought working through brush and pencil is in question.

In our general estimate of recent American art, we can affirm that only one thing is lacking to it: the appreciative support and sympathy of its own nation, publicly declared by critics, and, above all, attested by public patronage—for this is the only test of approval and the only condition of future existence and survival.

It would be absurd to allow patriotism to control or suggest our preferences in art. No more foolish thing could be suggested than to patronize American art simply because it is American. There is a better reason than patriotism or national pride for the appreciation of American art, which is that it deserves appreciation. But all good and genuine art presupposes a relationship between buyer and seller, a community of interests and thoughts. This relationship and this community are mainly dependent upon local contact, upon affinities of literature and language and daily life, upon a common basis of education. National art is not to be encouraged because it is national, but because no other art can take its place.

In recent American architecture the progress affirmed for sculpture and for painting has been fully equaled and perhaps surpassed.

It is in decorative art that American pre-eminence has asserted itself in the most distinct and emphatic way. Out-

FIG. 202.—The Fisherman and the Geni. From "The Arabian Nights." By Elihu Vedder. Photographed for this work at the Columbian Exposition, by permission of the Artist and Owner.

side of Japan or China there is no such school of ceramic decoration in modern art as can be found in the private circles of Cincinnati. I do not speak of the Rookwood pottery alone, which has originally developed from the style and work of a single amateur. Cincinnati is full of original talent in this direction. In its Museum the masterpieces of these amateurs are exhibited, with their dates. The work of Miss McLaughlin is possibly better known in Europe than it is here, although her name is a household word with all experts in decoration. The wood-carvings of Cincinnati have also wide renown, especially as connected with the family name of Fry. In decorative needlework the New York School of Mrs. Wheeler (Associated Artists) is distinctly superior to that of South Kensington in London. In stained glass the names of John La Farge, of Crowninshield, and of Louis Tiffany, are of epoch-making significance for all modern art. The architectural mosaics of the latter are a revival of the best qualities of the Byzantine, and it is doubtful if they have any rivals of importance in modern Europe.

FIG. 203.—Delilah. By Elihu Vedder. Photographed for this work at the Columbian Exposition, by permission of the Artist and Owner.

INDEX.

[A few pronunciations of foreign names have been entered in the text. The larger number will be found in the Index.]

The following definitions of technical terms used in the text may be useful to readers previously unfamiliar with the subject treated:

BUTTRESS : A masonry abutment strengthening a wall and placed at right angles to its surface.

CAPITAL : The decorative head of a column or pier.

CORNICE : Originally, in Greek architecture, a decorative roof line in stone, or the continuation of this roof line under the pediment. As copied, together with the entablature, by the Romans, this cornice frequently appears without relation to a roof line.

ENGAGED COLUMN : A column attached to a wall surface and used simply for decoration, not for support.

ENTABLATURE : The double lintel, with cornice, originally used in Greek architecture, thence copied by the Romans, and revived by the Italian Renaissance from the Roman use.

FRESCO : A painting on fresh or wet plaster, a term applied to wall-paintings in general.

IMPOST : A cube-shaped member occasionally placed over the capital of a column which supports an arch, in order to enlarge the supporting surface.

ORDER : This word is used traditionally and technically to specify (*a*) the Greek columnar style of architecture with its entablature, (*δ*) any one of the different styles in which the Greek columns and entablature appear.

PEDIMENT : (*a*) the gable of a Greek temple, (*δ*) the ornamental copy of such a gable form, (*c*) the ornamental curved variant of the gable form. See Fig. 20.

PIER : An architectural support constructed of aggregated masonry, not limited as to shape, whereas a column is always round.

GREEK ARCHITECTURE AND SCULPTURE.

By SMITH AND REDFORD.   12mo, cloth, 50 cents.

A carefully prepared volume, the work of two British scholars.   Edited by Prof. William H. Goodyear.   Illustrated with one hundred diagrams and drawings.

RENAISSANCE AND MODERN ART.

By Prof. WILLIAM H. GOODYEAR.   Chautauqua Edition,
12mo, cloth, $1.00.   *Edition de luxe*, printed on
heavy plate paper, illustrated with two hundred engravings reproduced largely from works of art on
exhibition at the Columbian Exposition.   Bound uniform with Roman and Medieval Art, in buckram cloth,
gilt top.   12mo, 310 pages, $2.00.

ROMAN AND MEDIEVAL ART.

By Prof. WILLIAM H. GOODYEAR.   Chautauqua Edition,
cloth, $1.00.   *Edition de luxe*, printed on heavy
coated paper, bound in buckram cloth, gilt top.
12mo, 250 pages, $2.00.

In this volume Prof. Goodyear, whose style is delightfully simple and readable, has traced the evolution of Greek art through Roman history into the Middle Ages.   The text is richly illustrated with 150 pictures of famous art treasures.

"An excellent manual of Roman and medieval art. . . . The book is profusely illustrated, and most of the illustrations are fresh in choice of subject and good in execution."—*The Outlook.*

"Written with a grasp of its subject that is not common with books of its kind. Mr. Goodyear knows what history and scholarship are; his facts are well selected and well arranged, and his statement of them is trustworthy. . . . The abundant process illustrations are very well chosen and well executed."—*The Nation.*

*** *Sent postpaid on receipt of price by the publishers.*

FLOOD & VINCENT, MEADVILLE, PA.

THE FOUR GEORGES.

By WILLIAM MAKEPEACE THACKERAY. The text is embellished with decorations, portraits, and vignettes of beautiful design by Mr. George Wharton Edwards. Printed in two colors. Large 8vo, richly bound in buff and white vellum, stamped in gold, with wide margins, flat back, rough edges, and gilt top. $3.00.

Thackeray's lectures on the Georgian reigns have usually been published in connection with other of his shorter pieces, and in consequence have often failed to receive the attention of the general reader. These pictures of English life in the eighteenth century are so charming, piquant, and accurate that Messrs. Flood & Vincent determined to give *The Four Georges* a new and distinctive edition.

The *Critic* pronounces this the finest edition of Thackeray's lectures on the Georgian reigns ever published on either side of the Atlantic. These essays of the famous English satirists are too often neglected by the general public. With the confidence that they would be appreciated, the publishers employed all the devices known to the printers' art in producing a rich and superb volume. Mr. Edwards' illustrations and decorations conform to the spirit of the age which the text describes, and are a most important contribution to the total effect of the book.

"This book compares very favorably with any of the beautiful volumes of its class which recent months have seen."—*The Nassau Literary Magazine.*

"The present publishers have given us a notably beautiful volume. We do not see what they could have done to make it more attractive."—*Nashville Advocate.*

"These papers were never put in a more becoming garb than this."—*The Book Buyer.*

"The book is one of the most attractive and best ever put out by an American firm."—*The Inlander.*

"It is very durably and handsomely bound, and a most charming book to present to a friend, especially if he is a lover of the beauties of Thackeray."—*Zion's Herald.*

₊ *Sent postpaid on receipt of price by the publishers.*

FLOOD & VINCENT, MEADVILLE, PA.

www.ingramcontent.com/pod-product-compliance
Lightning Source LLC
Chambersburg PA
CBHW031359270326

41929CB00010BA/1252